writing for the web

CREATING COMPELLING WEB CONTENT USING WORDS, PICTURES AND SOUND

LYNDA FELDER

New Riders
VOICES THAT MATTER™

Writing for the Web
Creating Compelling Web Content Using Words, Pictures and Sound
Lynda Felder

New Riders
1249 Eighth Street
Berkeley, CA 94710
510/524-2178
510/524-2221 (fax)

Find us on the Web at www.newriders.com
To report errors, please send a note to errata@peachpit.com

New Riders is an imprint of Peachpit, a division of Pearson Education
Copyright © 2012 by Lynda Felder

Associate Editor: Valerie Witte
Production Editor: Danielle Foster
Developmental Editor: Anne Marie Walker
Copyeditor: Anne Marie Walker
Proofreader: Scout Festa
Composition: Danielle Foster
Indexer: Joy Dean Lee
Cover Design: Charlene Charles-Will
Interior Design: Charlene Charles-Will and Danielle Foster

Photo Credits
Photo of Cuneiform script on clay tablet is in the public domain.
All other photos by Yashwin Chauhan. © Yashwin Chauhan. All rights reserved.

ISBN-13: 978-0-321-79443-7
ISBN-10:   0-321-79443-5
9 8 7 6 5 4 3 2 1
Printed and bound in the United States of America

For my sister, Carol

Acknowledgments

I would like to thank and acknowledge several people for their support in writing this book.

From Peachpit, Valerie Witte, who supported the idea of this book and kept it moving forward; Anne Marie Walker, who skillfully edited with just the right mix of demands and encouragement; designers Charlene Will and Danielle Foster, who made the pages look so inviting; and the rest of the impressive team.

Platt College students, who often make the classroom magical with their artistic focus and playful nature. The faculty and staff, who generously share their time and knowledge; and the dean, Marketa Hancova, for her leadership and inspiration.

My siblings, Marilyn and David, whom I can always count on.

My husband, Yashwin, who is not only an amazing photographer, but a constant source of amusement, strength, and support.

Contents

Chapter 4

Adding Motion   45

Chapter 5

Adding Sound   57

Chapter 6

Writing Nonlinear, Interactive Stories   73

Chapter 7

Writing Succinctly   83

| Chapter 12 | **Writing Blogs** | **141** |

| Chapter 13 | **Re-vision** | **153** |

| Chapter 14 | **Writing Practice** | **165** |

Start Here

Think about the last gadget you bought. If you're like most people, you felt a rush of excitement when you opened the package and couldn't wait to get your hands on the new toy. It's highly unlikely that you thought about reading the manual before you started pressing buttons and playing with your new purchase.

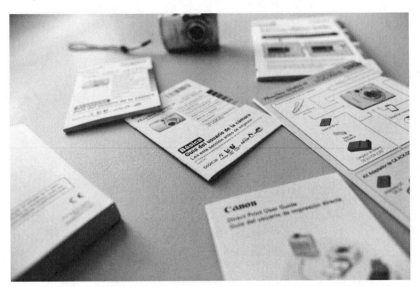

Don't Make Me Read

When a new object comes into your life, you simply want to point it in the right direction and make it work. The "point-and-shoot mentality" extends to everything, not just new gadgets. If the product's design is not intuitive, you're likely to think the designer was stupid or overzealous.

The same is true for Web content. When readers land on a Web page, they're not looking for *Instructions for Use*. Most don't have much time, and most don't have patience. Readers just want to land on the right page, instantly find what they're looking for, and then zoom off. When they stumble onto long paragraphs, when the text is unclear or boring, or when they find themselves studying, searching, or backtracking, they jump ship and head back to Google to search for better content.

> **HOW PEOPLE READ A WEB PAGE**
>
> In 1997, Jakob Nielsen pointed out that people don't typically read text on a Web page word for word. Rather, they scan, picking out words and phrases that are helpful. See Jakob Nielsen's October 1997 Alertbox column "How Users Read on the Web," which is available at www.useit.com.

Why You *Should* Read This Book

Most likely, you picked up this book because you want to better your skills at writing Web content. With many books available about this topic, why should you read this book?

- It's a thin book. Fat books typically don't follow their own guidelines, such as "be succinct"!

- It's designed to allow you to zoom in to find what you need, and then quickly skip to another topic.

- It encourages you to engage, to observe, to think, and to try various effective writing tasks. The chapters are packed with examples, challenges, and suggestions.

- It focuses on words, pictures, and sounds as story elements for your Web content rather than the mechanics of using specific software and tools. There's already a flood of good books available on how to use the latest tools and technology to capture and publish media. (You'll find suggestions for good books to read at www.write4web.com.)

How to Read This Book

As you read this book, you'll find there are no rules except to follow your own instincts. You'll get the most out of the book if you take breaks from reading to try the suggestions and challenges.

Challenges

At the end of each chapter, you'll find challenges that include writing prompts for freewriting and suggested exercises that will take more time.

Make sure you spend time on your own writing practice. As with any other discipline, the only way to get better at Web writing is to put in the time composing Web content. The art of creating compelling Web content is similar to any other art. You can't learn to dance by watching ballerinas. You can't learn to play the piano by listening to lectures or reading sheet music. Although it's

try this

Every chapter is peppered with "Try this" suggestions. Don't ignore these suggestions. You'll get the most out of this book if you pause, put down the book, and try the ideas offered. You'll learn the most if you decide right now to try everything with a playful spirit and an open mind.

helpful to listen with a keen ear to the music you enjoy, that won't place the magic in your fingertips. A pianist practices scales. A pianist plays finger exercises. A talented pianist spends hours and hours at the keyboard. A talented Web writer practices writing.

Consider all the suggestions, writing prompts, and assignments in this book as part of your finger exercises and part of your practice, moving you toward passionate, exciting Web stories.

More Information

You can find additional resources for *Writing for the Web* at www.write4web.com, including:

- **Additional challenges.** More freewriting and suggested exercises for your writing practice.
- **Evaluation criteria.** Suggestions for critiquing different types of Web writing.
- **Resources.** Web sites that are good examples or provide helpful information, reading lists, book reviews, and additional technical instructions.
- **Student work.** Examples of student blogs and podcasts.
- **Teacher notes.** A downloadable booklet with suggestions for teachers.

1

All You Really Need to Know

You've taken on a challenge that is exciting and fun, yet daunting—writing for the Web. The tools and technology are incredible and allow you to tell stories by mixing in any combination of multiple media—words, pictures (including photos, illustrations, graphics, animation, and video), and sound. You can also add opportunities for your reader to interact with your stories by providing polls, surveys, places to comment, and links to more information. The possibilities are unlimited.

There are so many choices to make. What will you write about? What do you want your reader to take away from your story, to take action on, to learn, or to understand? What media is the best fit for your story? How will you draw in your reader? How will you make sure that your story gets noticed? How will you keep your reader involved in the story?

Before all the exciting possibilities and challenges make you dizzy, take a deep breath. Then read this chapter to learn:

- How to make sure your story has three key features that will keep your readers' attention and ensure that they don't become confused, bored, or disinterested
- How to determine who your audience is
- How to stay on target, delivering the right content for your audience

Messages, Messages, Messages

There's a message waiting for you at any place or any time. Even while you're hiking in Molokai (**FIGURE 1.1**)!

FIGURE 1.1

Everywhere you turn there are messages.

As you go about your daily business, you are barraged with countless messages and instructions. Walk, don't run. Don't point. Be a good neighbor. Be a good citizen. Wash your hands. No spitting (**FIGURE 1.2**). Yield the right of way. Stop. Go. Quiet!

What makes you accept some messages as truths and others as hogwash? What makes you accept some instructions as the right thing to do and reject others?

FIGURE 1.2

And more messages.

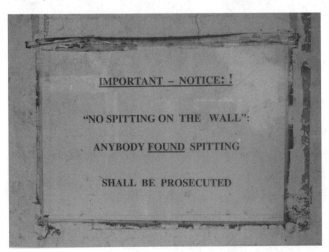

Discovering what motivates you to pay attention is helpful in figuring out what will hold your readers' attention.

Messages on the Web

On the Web you'll also find a constant deluge of messages and instructions:

- Read me
- Buy me
- Click me
- Sign up for me

But you are not forced to follow any of the advice or instructions that appear on your screen. As much as various ads and treatises on the Web try to get in your face, you are the one in control. You choose what you will hold on to and explore and what you will let go. And you can shut it all down in an instant when you run out of time, get bored, or feel overwhelmed. This is a comforting thought unless you are writing for the Web and don't want your messages to be turned off and shut down.

Let's consider how viewers approach the fluid chaos of the Web and sort through the myriad pieces of information to find exactly what suits their current needs.

Web Soup

The Web is a huge, soupy mess filled with stories and messages that are

- Fascinating
- Boring
- Eye-opening
- Scary
- Incredulous
- Beautiful
- Ugly
- Superficial
- Complicated
- Hideous
- Brilliant
- Stupid
- Distasteful
- Unintelligible
- Confusing
- All of the above and more

At every moment in time, more and more ugly, shocking, gruesome, dull, exotic, and wonderful stories are added to the broth.

Web readers dip into this liquid mess with the help of various utensils, or search engines. If they find what they want, they try it out. If they find something that doesn't match their tastes and needs, they throw it back into the soup and dip in again.

Think for a moment about the last time you were on the Internet. What were you looking for? What actions did you take? What made you pay attention? What made you ignore one story or a Web page in its entirety and move on to

Be obscure clearly! Be wild of tongue in a way we can understand!

—E.B. White

something else? What enticed you? What made you look for more? What was so good that you bookmarked it or told a friend about it?

As a Web reader, it can be difficult to determine why you choose one story over another. Your needs, your drives, your wants, your dreams, your ambitions, and your sense of who you are can change at any given point in time. What you wanted as a child is different from what you want now. What you wanted yesterday can change dramatically tomorrow. Yet there is always some reason you feel compelled to choose one story over another.

As a Web author, you want to make sure that your Web content and messages reach the needs and desires of your intended readers and make them pay attention.

Make Your Messages Rise Above the Din

To make sure that your Web content gets noticed, you need to write about topics that will get sorted out of the soup and taste good to your readers. So how can you make your Web stories so appetizing that your readers will keep coming back for more? Your content must have the following three characteristics:

CLARITY   SPARK   MEANING

Make Your Content Clear

Your content must be clear and obvious to readers. If it's obtuse, confusing, complicated, or unintelligible, you'll lose readers' attention.

What's the purpose of your content? If you don't know, your content probably won't be clear.

What are the key messages that you want your readers to take away? If you don't know, your content probably won't be clear.

Who is the content written for? If you don't know,...

In the following sections, you'll find a few common problems that can make your content hard to understand, along with suggestions for fixes.

SHAGGY DOG STORIES

Shaggy dog refers to a story that winds and weaves on and on with one tangent after another. Your readers can't discern the direction or focus and wonder when the story will end and what the point was.

You can fix this problem by writing down the main messages and key points of your story. You should be able to state what the content is about in three sentences or less.

Consider the following shaggy dog story and possible solutions.

Write an elevator pitch for your story. An *elevator pitch* is a summary of the story that you can say in about 30 seconds, the time it takes for an average elevator ride. Your pitch should make someone want to read the story.

AIMLESS STORY	SOLUTIONS
Clarissa and her husband, Jeremy, were married six months when Clarissa came home with a dog she had rescued from the animal shelter. The dog, named Max, had a few bad habits. He liked the taste of leather and chewed up several pairs of Clarissa's and Jeremy's shoes. He also slept on the couch, which was not allowed, when no one was looking. Clarissa's mother pointed out that the carpet needed vacuuming, and that Sears had a sale on vacuums. Jeremy lost his job. Then Jeremy had to stay home and make sure Max didn't eat shoes and sleep on the couch.	Decide what the story is about, remove all the tangential information, and relate the sequence of events that tell the main story you have in mind. For example, perhaps the story is about Clarissa's mother interfering. Or maybe it's about newlyweds who want to have children and decide to try out their parenting skills on a dog first. Or maybe it's about Jeremy losing his job and feeling like Max's nanny.

TIME TRAVELING WITHOUT THE MACHINE

A time traveling story madly swerves in time. It shifts tenses within a single sentence. It jumps from present to past to future without any transitions or warnings. Your readers will feel like they've been in a car race without a seatbelt.

You can fix this problem by sticking to past tense and not flashing back or forward in time.

Consider the following time traveling sentence and the possible solution.

TENSE SHIFTS	SOLUTION
After I visit my friend Carly, I decided I wanted to travel and see the world.	After I visited my friend Carly, I decided I wanted to travel and see the world.

FOGGY VISION

A foggy vision story has vague and general language or images. The content isn't explicit or specific. The detail is high level, and readers can't get a clear picture of what is going on.

You can fix this problem by knowing the specific terms and details your readers are familiar with and by using concrete nouns and active verbs to paint a vivid story.

Consider the following example and possible solution.

VAGUE AND GENERAL TERMS	SOLUTION
Kristie was happy that her dad bought her a vehicle for graduation.	Kristie danced around the red VW bug her dad had just given her for graduation.

STREAM-OF-CONSCIOUSNESS THINKING

A stream-of-consciousness story follows a logic only known to you, the author, because you simply spat out everything that was in your head and heart and did not take the time to think of how your audience would follow the thoughts and ideas. Freewriting is an effective way to brainstorm and get a story started. But after the initial draft, you'll need to reorganize the content in a way that makes sense to your reader. Very few authors can get away with publishing their first drafts. Jack Kerouac's incredible, exciting stories rolled off his typewriter without revision. But this talent came with years of intense study.

You can often spot stream-of-consciousness Web content in the first sentence. When authors begin with a tentative statement or seem to have several starts before making any sense or point, you can tell that they posted their very first outpouring without any attempt to revise the piece.

Although the following example is exaggerated to make a point, you can probably find a blog post on the Internet that begins just as tentatively.

STREAM-OF-CONSCIOUSNESS	POSSIBLE SOLUTION
I'm not big on writing blogs, and I wasn't sure what to write about. I am writing this blog for my assignment. I spent a lot of time looking around our apartment for something to come to me. Then I saw Fishbreath, our cat. Fishbreath almost died more than once. I decided to write about her near-death experiences.	Our cat, Fishbreath, has already lived nine lives.

CONFUSING LANGUAGE

At the sentence level, a story might contain misplaced modifiers, unclear pronouns, vague terminology, or ambiguous statements. Sometimes your readers will get a big laugh, because the confusion makes the sentence comical.

Consider the following sentences and possible corrections.

UNCLEAR PRONOUN	CLEAR SENTENCE
Jane told Ginny that her boyfriend was amusing.	Jane said, "Ginny, your boyfriend is amusing."

MISPLACED MODIFIER	CLEAR SENTENCE
Dressed with balsamic vinegar, Doug brought a salad to the potluck.	Doug brought a salad with a balsamic vinegar dressing to the potluck.

Give Your Content Spark

Everyone knows what it's like to produce a dull, sleep-inducing story. Most likely, it happens when you are barely awake as you are writing it.

If, as you are developing your content, you feel it lacks spark, take a break. Try to recall a movie that you were totally lost in. Think of a game or a song that was so seductive that you forgot where you were. Consider a TV show that you didn't want to end—a series that you recorded because you couldn't wait to watch the next episode. Then think about these questions:

- What drew you in?
- How did it start?
- Was there a cliff-hanger?
- Was there a puzzle?
- Was there danger?
- How did it end?

The more you know about what excites you, the more you will be able to add spark to your own content.

Consider the following sentence with no spark and the possible solution.

NO SPARK	SPARK
Some ideas came to me the other day, and I have finally come up with a plan and a vision.	I have a dream.

Make Sure Your Content Matters

If you write about a subject that only you and your mother might find mildly interesting, you'll bore your readers, and they'll move on.

If you write about topics that are the equivalent of humdrum daily routines, like brushing your teeth or eating breakfast, you need to step away from the keyboard and reenvision what topics inspire you. What are your passions? What motivates you? What is it that you care deeply about?

The key to ensuring that your Web content has clarity, spark, and meaning is to understand yourself and to understand your audience.

Who Is Your Audience?

When someone asks you who you are writing for, there's a temptation to say, "Everyone!" Everyone will be interested in this particular topic. But this is not a good idea. If you try to meet everyone's needs, your content will be too broad and too general. It won't have a clear drive, solid organization, or inviting details. The most exciting topic for an octogenarian will most likely not work for a tween. Neither of these age groups is likely to have an interest in how to clean an oven or find a nanny.

If you've been to Toastmasters or taken a speech class, you've learned that it's best to gear your talk toward one person or a group of people in the audience rather than the multitudes. It's the same way with developing Web content. When you have in mind a particular person or group, the language, the details, the organization, the examples, the anecdotes, and the other parts of your content fit the expectations and tastes of someone rather than no one.

If your readers are not obvious, how can you determine who your audience is? You can start by making lists of all your favorite activities. What excites you? For each item, think of others who would also care about the activity.

For example, let's say you are crazy about snowboarding and have decided to design a blog site for snowboarding enthusiasts. Make a list of any friends and associates who also love to snowboard. Add to the list names of snowboarders you've seen on TV or read about. This is just a starting point.

You'll then need to gather information about your audience.

Get to Know Your Audience

Once you have a general idea of who your audience is and have made a list of specific members of that group, you'll have many ways to get to know your audience better.

If you are writing about a subject that is near and dear to your heart, you'll have a huge head start on who your readers are and what topics they will like. Here are a few suggestions to gather information:

- Ask questions (phone, email, text, etc.).
- Attend events (tradeshows, competitions, forums, etc.).
- Watch TV and YouTube interviews of more famous people.
- Read blogs or news stories.

Sometimes, however, you might be tasked to write for a group that you don't know well. Let's say, for example, that you've just begun working in a biomedical company and you are tasked to write instructional guides for pharmacists. You know that you need to focus only on pharmacists working in hospitals, not those working in other environments, such as drugstores. Here are a few ways in which you can try to get to know your audience:

- Meet with pharmacists at their workplace. Take note of the space, the furniture, any equipment, the colors, the smells.

- Ask questions. What is a typical day like? What are the biggest concerns? What are the roadblocks? What or who is most helpful? What are typical scenarios for tasks?

- Read literature targeted for this group.

- Talk to others who interact with this group. Does the company have a customer service department? What sort of calls does customer service get?

- Volunteer to work for customer service or provide another service for the group.

> *When genuine passion moves you, say what you've got to say, and say it hot.*
>
> —D.H. Lawrence

The main idea is to interact, ask appropriate questions, and obtain information to better identify your readers and know their interests, issues, and needs.

Develop a Persona

The word persona has different meanings, depending on the context. For Web design, usability, and Web content, a persona is a hypothetical user or reader. The persona is a made-up person but is based on real details gathered from real people in your targeted audience.

Let's say you have been hired to develop content for an organization that wants to promote healthy outdoor activities for retired seniors. Part of developing the persona involves finding a picture of someone who looks like your typical reader (**FIGURE 1.3**).

FIGURE 1.3
Find an image representative of your key audience.

ALAN COOPER AND PERSONAS

Alan Cooper first introduced the design tool called a persona in his book *The Inmates Are Running the Asylum* (Sams, 2009). Personas are now a popular tool used for usability, Web design, and other formats where it's important to understand the audience. A persona is a hypothetical user, a model, or archetype, based on information and details collected from real people.

After you have collected all the information you need about your audience, you can easily create the persona to help you stay on track and write to a specific type of person.

To help you identify with your persona, you'll choose a fictional name. Then, you just need to create a short bio for that hypothetical person.

You can use the template shown in **FIGURE 1.4** to design the persona.

Name _____

Demographics:
    Age
    Occupation
    Income Range
    City

A brief sketch with descriptive details about
Web usage, likes, and dislikes. Include typical
scenarios.

FIGURE 1.4
Develop a persona.

Use your persona to help judge whether or not your Web content appeals to
your targeted audience. Make sure that the content is clear, has spark, and mat-
ters to your reader.

Challenges

The best way to get better at writing Web content is to write, write some more,
and rewrite. The challenges in this chapter concentrate on understanding your
audience as well as yourself.

Freewriting

The freewriting challenges ask you to write for distinctly different audiences and
to reflect on your word choice, topics, themes, mood, pace, and tone.

Freewriting works best when it is timed. If you tend to write quickly, set the timer
for ten minutes. If you tend to take a little more time, give yourself 15 minutes.
Remember that with freewriting you don't need to worry about accuracy, grammar, spelling, and so forth. The practice is about capturing your first thoughts.

FIRST THOUGHTS

In 1986, Natalie Goldberg introduced what is now commonly referred to
as *freewriting*. In her landmark book *Writing Down the Bones* (Shambhala,
2010), Goldberg referred to freewriting as first thoughts and writing practice. One of the rules for freewriting is to keep your hand moving for the
allotted time. Of course, Goldberg was talking about writing with a pen
and notebook. For Web writing, you must keep both hands moving as you
type on the keyboard.

WRITE A LETTER TO GRANNY

Write a letter to your grandmother. If writing a letter to your grandmother doesn't resonate with you, try writing a letter to any older relative in your family—an aunt or an uncle.

After you write the letter, make a note of the following:

- Your choice of topics
- Your tone
- The language you used
- Your feelings and moods
- The pace of the letter
- Whether you wrote fast or slow
- The length of the letter

TEXT A BUDDY

Send an actual text message to someone you're buddies with who is about your age. Record all the same writing details listed in "Write a letter to granny."

MY GENERATION

List three words that describe your generation. Then write two paragraphs telling why you chose those words.

Suggested Exercises

Exercises are longer projects that will take more time to complete. You can find more complete instructions, learning outcomes, and criteria for critiquing your work at www.write4web.com.

1. For three days, keep an activity log of how and why you surfed the Web. What were you looking for? What were your activities? What topics did you search? Did you buy anything? What intrigued you? What annoyed you?

2. Create a persona, based on the earlier discussion in "Developing a Persona," for a specific audience and subject you enjoy. If you're not sure what you want to write about, read Chapter 12, "Writing Blogs," for suggestions.

3. Write a blog entry or essay called *Self-reflection*. Describe your skills as a writer and what you would like to improve. Talk about the type of work you do or what you are studying in school. Tell what topics interest you.

Up Next

Now that you know you need to add clarity, spark, and meaning to your writing, and you've learned how to get to know your audience, you can move on to learn more effective skills to enhance your writing. Chapter 2, "Best Practices for Writing for the Web," provides proven techniques that give your work professionalism and polish.

2

Best Practices for Writing for the Web

Because reading on the Web is such a different experience than reading printed literature, it only makes sense that your techniques for Web writing will also be different. If you are one of the lucky students who have had a good writing teacher at some point in your schooling, you probably already have some fantastic skills and techniques that work well for your writing. However, you might need to rethink and revamp some of your methods. Sometimes learning a new skill set involves forgetting knowledge and skills that you learned in the past, because they no longer serve your needs.

Of course, some advice for good writing applies to both printed and electronic media—for example, using precise language, active voice, and plain terms.

This chapter walks you through techniques that will ensure that your writing is designed for Web reading. Guidelines contained in this chapter will help you make your story more:

- Elegant
- Professional
- Understandable
- Expressive
- Readable

Write Succinctly

Write clean, active sentences. Crisp, snappy sentences attract and hold your readers' attention.

> **BE SUCCINCT!**
>
> Web guru Jakob Nielsen published his timeless article "Be Succinct! (Writing for the Web)" in 1997, and it's still widely read today. You can find more usability tips and guidelines for Web writing from Nielsen at *www.useit.com*.

Because composing concise content is such an important practice for writing for the Web, an entire chapter is devoted to deleting unnecessary content. See Chapter 7, "Writing Succinctly," for more about how to make sure your content is tight and spare.

Cut Word Count by Half

For your first draft, don't concern yourself with how you write. Just jot down all your thoughts. After you have a draft that you feel is complete, then edit, ruthlessly. Smash, slash, and trash as many words as you can. Put even your favorite words and phrases on the cutting block. Some authors say that you should cut the word count by half, and then cut it in half again. That is a challenge!

Use a Conversational Style

A conversational style means writing like you are having a conversation. Write like you talk, only better. If you take on a writing style that does not feel real and natural, you will distance the reader from the piece. Check your style to see if it sounds like you, but with more panache. Make sure the story doesn't sound patronizing, avuncular, or pedantic. Make sure it doesn't sound like you are trying to impress someone.

The following example illustrates a pedantic style versus a more conversational style.

SAMPLE PEDANTIC STYLE	REVISION
Indeed, one would assume that the titular head of our family, the matriarch, manufactured the theological impression that she was of supernatural origins.	My grandmother thought she was a goddess.

IN THE FIELD WITH A BUDDY

Photographer Scott Kelby states in the beginning of *The Digital Photography Book* (Peachpit, 2007) that he is writing the book as though you, the reader, and he are out in the field on a photo shoot. You are asking him questions, and he is answering them, throughout the book. It's this conversational style, easy to read and understand, that helps makes his digital photography books so popular.

Sound Like You, Only Better

Your writing style should feel like something *you* would say if you could edit yourself while talking. The written conversation sounds more scripted. You need to distill the phrases so you don't repeat words, so you've chosen the most precise terms, and so the sentences flow together well rather than chopping along in fits and starts. You don't want the conversation to sound like small talk, like chit-chat, or as though you just got out of bed and answered the phone. You need to cut out all the uhs, ers, and ahems. You need to omit all the backpedaling and floundering you speak when you're trying to find your footing in the topic.

The following example illustrates small talk versus a distilled style.

SAMPLE SMALL TALK	REVISION
Hey dude. Yo. How's it hangin'? Man, what an awesome adventure! Still can't believe I spent a whole month in India. It was wild!	I spent the month of May exploring Rajasthan, India.

Take a walk in a public place or find a comfortable place to sit in a park or coffee shop. Listen in on the conversations you hear. Take notes. When you have enough material, take the time to rewrite the conversations in a conversational but distilled style.

Write with an Attitude

As you are writing about any topic, walk into it like it is Buckingham Palace and you own the place. A timid, self-effacing tone will turn off your reader.

The following example illustrates a timid style versus attitude.

SAMPLE TIMID SENTENCES	REVISION WITH ATTITUDE
Well, I think that being an artist and making money is a difficult issue that can be hard to work out. It seems like some artists are OK with the whole commercialism thing, and I believe it works out fine for them.	Ansel Adams thrived on his commercial adventures.

Use Precise Terms

Use words that best represent your meaning.

Using precise language involves not only enhancing your vocabulary so that you know the exact terms to use, but understanding the vocabulary that your audience is familiar with. If you are talking to car enthusiasts and want to mention a bouquet of flowers, it's probably enough to use the term "roses" when describing the flowers. However, if you are writing for the American Rose Society, you would mention a more specific name. For a white rose, you might mention a John F. Kennedy or a Queen Mary II.

LE SEUL MOT JUSTE

French writer Gustave Flaubert is famous for his first novel, *Madame Bovary* (Viking Adult, 2010), written in 1856. He is also famous for coining the phrase *le seul mot juste*, which means the one right word. Flaubert claims that he spent nights pacing the floor, agonizing over the one right word.

Keep Verbs Active

Print out a Web story you have written. Read through your sentences and highlight or circle any form of the verb "to be." Be sure to highlight all forms of the verb (to be, am, is, are, was, were, being, been, be). Then, rewrite each sentence that uses to be, substituting an active verb.

Sometimes vague or nondescriptive verbs slip into your writing when you use:

- Passive voice
- Instances of the verb "to be"
- Instances of other dull verbs, such as "do" or "got"

For more detailed information on how to avoid passive voice, see Chapter 11, "Writing Instructions."

While you're editing your work, identify those places where you've pumped up weaker verbs with adverbs. Delete them and revise weak sentences with strong verbs that clearly show the action.

The following example illustrates a sentence with weak verbs versus strong verbs.

SAMPLE WITH WEAK VERBS	REVISION
Mary was late, and she was running to her class to do her talk for the students.	Late, Mary raced to the classroom to speak to the students.

Show and Tell

Writers' books often advise you to *show, don't tell*. That means that instead of making general statements or providing an overview statement, you should provide a close point of view and paint a picture with details.

The following example illustrates telling versus showing.

TELLING	SHOWING
Jeff likes chocolate.	Jeff bit into the chocolate bar, closing his eyes and sighing as the dark sweetness melted on his tongue.

With Web writing, the best technique is often to show *and* tell. If you only describe detail after detail, readers have to work harder to discern the meaning. If you just tell, the content is flat and more abstract.

Use Specific Concrete Nouns

Use specific concrete nouns to help your readers paint detailed pictures in their heads. An abstract noun cannot be seen, heard, smelled, tasted, or felt, whereas a concrete noun can. Transportation is an abstract term, whereas motorcycle is concrete. To truly draw in your readers, use the specific concrete nouns that they will relate to and like. If your readers are bikers who like Harleys, the specific concrete noun that you use might be *Fat Boy*.

> *Don't tell me the moon is shining; show me the glint of light on broken glass.*
>
> —Anton Chekhov

Compare the following abstract, concrete, and specific concrete nouns.

ABSTRACT	CONCRETE	SPECIFIC CONCRETE
• Time	• Clock	• Cuckoo clock
• Fear	• Dog	• Chihuahua
• Bravado	• Tree	• Maple

Use Plain Terms

Use terms that are easy to understand and quick to read. Writing in plain English means that most of the words in your sentences are no longer than three syllables and that all of the words are comprehensible without a dictionary or lawyer by your side.

The following example illustrates pompous versus plain English.

NOT PLAIN ENGLISH	REVISED AS PLAIN ENGLISH
The extemporaneous discourse communicated by Shannon was acknowledged with approbation.	Shannon gave an impromptu speech that was well received.

OBJECTIVE CONSIDERATION

In his article "Politics and the English Language," included in *A Collection of Essays* (Mariner Books, 1970), George Orwell tells us that English is in a bad way. He takes a verse from *Ecclesiastes*, which is written plainly, and rewrites it in what he calls modern English.

The original verse reads:

"I returned and saw under the sun, that the race is not to the swift, nor the battle to the strong, neither yet bread to the wise, nor yet riches to men of understanding, nor yet favour to men of skill; but time and chance happeneth to them all."

The translated sentence reads:

"Objective considerations of contemporary phenomena compel the conclusion that success or failure in competitive activities exhibits no tendency to be commensurate with innate capacity, but that a considerable element of the unpredictable must invariably be taken into account."

Avoid Idioms

An idiom is a phrase or expression that is inherent to a particular culture, region, or people. The problem with idioms is that they don't often translate across cultures and regions. Take the following expression: *it's as easy as falling off a log*. If you know this expression, you understand that something is quite easy. Comparable expressions you might use include:

- It's a piece of cake.
- There's nothing to it.
- It's as easy as pie.
- It's a no-brainer.
- It's like taking candy from a baby.
- No sweat.

All of these expressions are idioms. If you were to translate, word for word, *it's as easy as falling off a log* into another language, such as German, the translation would confuse your reader. In German, the idiom is *kinderleicht ein Kinderspiel*, or *it's child's play*. In German, if you have *ein Haar in der Suppe* (a hair in the soup), you have something to kvetch about, just like *a fly in the ointment*.

You should avoid such idiomatic phrases because they are too much trouble for your readers to understand.

Spell Out Acronyms

If you love acronyms, you might get a citation by the AAAAA (American Association Against Acronym Abuse). All kidding aside, don't use an acronym unless you are absolutely sure that your readers will whiz past it without a second thought. Most of us know that 24/7 stands for 24 hours/7 days a week. But do you know what 24-D stands for? You'd probably have to look this one up. It is an acronym for 2,4-Dichlorophenoxyacetic acid.

The difference between the almost right word and the right word is really a large matter—'tis the difference between the lightning bug and the lightning.

—Mark Twain

Break Up Tangled Nouns

Sentences with several nouns jammed together, creating a tangle of compound nouns, are hard to read and can slow down readers to a standstill. Sometimes, even after reading the sentence a few times, they still might not be able to figure out what it means. You can find plenty of tangled nouns in newspapers; news editors create titles with nouns strung together to save space.

Here's an example: Fatal Alcohol-Related Officer Involved Shooting

This type of sentence needs revision, so that the sentence is easier to read. You'll need to add some of the smaller words, like prepositions, articles, conjunctions, and transitions to help guide the reader. The revised version is likely to have a higher word count. But more words, in this case, are preferable to a confusing tangle of nouns.

Consider the following tangled sentence and its more readable revision.

NOUN TANGLE	REVISION
The recruiter prescreened phone interviewed skill tested applicant was brought in for an interview.	The applicant was first prescreened by a recruiter and then interviewed by phone and given a skills test. Then we brought her in for an interview.

Be Wary of Trendy Terms

Trendy terms are only fun to use for a fleeting moment. After that moment, they become overused, and like a cliché, they bore the reader and give your sentences a lackluster tone and quality. If you're using a term that was trendy more than six months ago, your reader might not know what you're talking about.

Here are a couple of examples of trendy words:

- **Staycation**, which means having your vacation at home. This word is popular during economic downturns when vacationers need to economize.

- **Kerfuffle**, which means a disturbance or fuss. Kerfuffle is such a popular word in 2011 that *New York Times* blogger Phillip B. Corbett asks in his article "Words We Love Too Much," "Who flicked on the 'kerfuffle' switch?" (See Corbett's article at http://topics.blogs.nytimes.com/2011/04/19/words-we-love-too-much-6.)

DON'T BE PLUTOED

Every year the American Dialect Society chooses a Word of the Year (WotY). The word for 2010 was app. App is an abbreviation for application, a software program that works on your phone or computer (www.americandialect.org).

For 2006, the American Dialect Society chose plutoed as the Word of the Year. To be plutoed is to be demoted or devalued. That same year, the International Astronomical Union voted that Pluto could no longer be considered a planet; thus, Pluto was demoted to the status of dwarf planet.

If you use the word plutoed in 2011, you might lose your audience.

Make a list of every phrase you use, and those you've heard others use, that means, *I like it!* Write down who the audience is for each phrase. Don't forget these:

It's the cat's pajamas; it's the bee's knees; I'm over the moon about it; it's the bomb; and so on.

Another problem with trendy words is that they scream out the author's background and tastes, and ignore the reader. Which words do you use in conversation to say something is perfect and good? If you are British, you might say you were "well chuffed" if you really liked something. Americans, in the '70s, said "groovy" or "mellow." In the '90s the word "awesome" was popular. Be aware of the words you choose.

Use Foreign Phrases Sparingly

Foreign phrases can be trendy and sound snooty. They can also say just what you mean when an English phrase fails. *Joie de vivre* can set the tone and mood so much better than the word *exuberance* or the phrase *a healthy joy of life*. If you've just heard a phrase that you like on the radio or TV, chances are that that phrase has become in vogue and everyone will be trying it out. Case in point: While Hillary Clinton and Barack Obama were campaigning for president, reporters couldn't seem to resist the temptation to overuse the phrase *pas de deux*, which is a ballet term meaning a dance between two persons.

List Items

By using lists rather than straight text, you make information easier for your readers to scan and take in quickly. You also break up larger chunks of text, which can give your writing a heavier, bogged-down feeling.

The following example shows a sentence with items joined by commas versus a sentence that uses bullets for a list of items.

SAMPLE WITHOUT LIST	REVISION FOR EASIER READING
The largest fresh surface-water system on earth includes the Great Lakes: Michigan, Superior, Huron, Erie, and Ontario, and their connecting channels.	The following Great Lakes and their connecting channels form the largest fresh surface-water system on earth: • Michigan • Superior • Huron • Erie • Ontario

Use Bullets for Laundry Lists

If the items in a list you're referring to have no particular sequence, use bullet points rather than numbers. For example, if you need to list items that have spilled out of a box (**FIGURE 2.1**), list them with bullet points.

FIGURE 2.1
For items that are not sequenced, use bullet points.

The following example shows a list of items with no sequence.

SAMPLE BULLET POINTS
The contents of the junk box spilled out to reveal a • padlock • tube of lipstick • Christmas ornament • pen • napkin ring

Use Numbers for Sequences

Use numbers for items in a list that are sequential. For example, if you are writing instructions on how to perform a task with software, you need to follow a sequence.

The following example shows a list of sequential items.

ROTATE AN IMAGE IN PHOTOSHOP
1. With Photoshop running, open the image file. 2. From the menu bar, select Image. 3. Select Image rotation at 180°.

Keep Sentences Short

Keep sentences brief and to the point. If you've written a sentence that needs more than a comma or two, rethink it. Short, simple sentences are much easier to read and comprehend online. When your readers find convoluted sentences in printed literature, they can pause, reread, and take more time to digest the meaning.

If you like to use semicolons to join short sentences together, rethink this practice for three reasons. First, punctuation marks (semicolons, colons, commas, apostrophes) are hard to read online. Second, lengthy sentences are more difficult to read. Third, your readers do not have the patience to sort out complicated meanings.

Avoid Run-on Sentences

A common mistake beginning writers make is to jam several sentences together without any punctuation. If punctuation is used, it is often a comma that separates complete sentences. For the reader, it feels like the author has spilled out several thoughts without taking a breath. This mistake is called a *run-on sentence*, because the sentence runs along, jamming complete thoughts and sentences together without any periods.

If you are revising a run-on sentence for printed literature, you can join two or more short, related sentences with semicolons. On the Web, however, semicolons are harder to see. And shorter, simpler sentences separated by periods and spaces are much easier to read.

Consider how you might revise the following sentence for print and for the Web.

SAMPLE RUN-ON	REVISION FOR PRINT	REVISION FOR WEB
Mary went to the grocery store, she needed to buy milk, she had invited her friends Sally and Jerry over for breakfast, Sally and Jerry like to drink coffee with milk.	Mary went to the grocery store; she needed milk. She had invited her friends Sally and Jerry over for breakfast.	Mary went to the store for milk. Her friends Sally and Jerry were coming over for breakfast.

Use Simple Sentence Structures

Consider this long, unwieldy sentence from the Declaration of Independence:

"We hold these truths to be self-evident, that all men are created equal, that they are endowed by their Creator with certain unalienable Rights, that among these are Life, Liberty and the pursuit of Happiness."

If our forefathers had written this for the Web, they might have revised it to say:

We hold these truths as self-evident. All are created equal. All have certain unalienable Rights. Among the rights are

- Life
- Liberty
- Pursuit of Happiness

Strip each sentence to its cleanest components.

—William Zinsser, On Writing Well

For printed content, readers are more likely to follow a complex thought process. With a book, for example, it's easy to flip back a few pages to reread and absorb content. But on the Web, remember that your reader is typically in a hurry and not prone to reflection or study. The reader darts around on the page and only lands on each sentence for a moment. Short, easy sentences work best.

Keep Paragraphs Short

In a Basic Composition writing course, you learn how to build paragraphs of substance. Sometimes the teacher might say that one of your paragraphs is too wimpy—that it doesn't have enough meat. The teacher might also say that the paragraph needs at least 75 words in order to say something. You are told that your paragraphs are building blocks, and you are taught to add layers and substance to each of your building blocks with details, anecdotes, examples, scenarios, dialogue, or elaborate description. If you are writing for the Web, this is one of those lessons that you can and need to unlearn.

On the Web you can write paragraphs that have only one or two sentences. Just make sure that there's a specific topic in each paragraph.

Use One Topic Per Paragraph

Include only one topic per paragraph in your writing to keep the content concise, well organized, and easy to group with like topics. Begin with the topic sentence and follow with information that supports that topic. When your paragraphs follow a simple structure, the content is easier for your readers to take in. The content is also easier for you or the site's information architect to manage.

Begin with a Strong Lead

If you've taken a traditional writing class, you were taught to begin your paragraphs with an interesting hook, a *topic sentence*, and then follow it with several sentences that build to the ending sentence. The topic sentence is the only important sentence in the paragraph because it states what the paragraph is about.

For Web writing, the best practice is to use a paragraph structure called the *inverted pyramid* (**FIGURE 2.2**). The inverted pyramid turns the traditional paragraph upside down. It begins with a topic sentence, which states what the paragraph is about, and then the most critical and interesting content follows. For years, journalists have been using the inverted pyramid for newspaper reporting.

A big benefit of leading your paragraph with the most important information is that this is what appears before a Read More link. If you start your paragraph with generalizations, the reader will see only fluff and will most likely not click Read More.

Wouldn't it be nice if you could click Read Less?

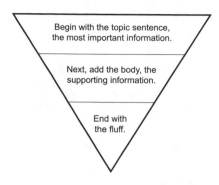

FIGURE 2.2
The inverted pyramid.

Chunk Information

For Web content, it's best to chunk information into smaller topics or sets of topics that can be easily grouped and organized. Chunking also makes it simpler to plan how you'll link topics together. With printed text, readers can readily flip back a few pages to read material again. Online, however, readers more easily lose their train of thought and aren't as likely to return to pages they've already passed.

Organize content so the chunks of information can stand on their own as much as possible. Also, keep in mind that viewers don't want to read long pages of text onscreen. Many also don't like to scroll, so consider this as you plan links and how information will appear to your readers.

Compare the following two blog posts for a good and bad example of chunking information (**FIGURES 2.3** and **2.4**).

Using Dashes, Hyphens, and Colons

Posted on June 4, 2011 by Chelsea

Use dashes to emphasize or set apart comments in your sentences. A pair of dashes functions like parentheses. A single dash functions like a colon. The dash, however, is less formal and more dramatic. Never use a hyphen (-) in place of a dash (—). It's just wrong and looks incredibly wimpy. The wrong way to punctuate is: We evacuated-the neighborhood was on fire! The right way to punctuate is: We evacuated—the neighborhood was on fire!

Use hyphens for compound words and to hyphenate words at the end of a line. For example: T-shirt, well-known, sixty-five. Use a colon to introduce a related idea or items within a sentence. For example, Seaside College students have a choice of the following disciplines: video, 3D animation, web, and print design. If the sentence has two independent clauses that are related, separate the independent clauses with a semicolon. For example, Seaside College students have many choices; they can study video, 3D animation, web, or print design.

FIGURE 2.3
Content is not organized into chunks.

Using Dashes, Hyphens, and Colons

Posted on June 4, 2011 by Chelsea

Dashes

Use dashes to emphasize or set apart comments in your sentences. A pair of dashes functions like parentheses. A single dash functions like a colon. The dash, however, is less formal and more dramatic.

Never use a hyphen (-) in place of a dash (—). It's just wrong and looks incredibly wimpy.

- INCORRECT: We evacuated-the neighborhood was on fire!
- CORRECT: We evacuated—the neighborhood was on fire!

Hyphens

Use hyphens for compound words and to hyphenate words at the end of a line. For example: T-shirt, well-known, sixty-five.

Colons

Use a colon to introduce a related idea or items within a sentence. For example, Seaside College students have a choice of the following disciplines: video, 3D animation, web, and print design.

If the sentence has two independent clauses that are related, separate the independent clauses with a semicolon. For example, Seaside College students have many choices; they can study video, 3D animation, web, or print design.

Title and Subtitle

Use titles and subtitles to break up long sections of text and to make topics scannable. Make sure your titles are clear and easy to read. Write meaningful titles that match your readers' expectations. Avoid cute, clever, vague (**FIGURE 2.5**), or alliterative titles that try to impress. You want your titles to act as signposts for the content.

Scared?

Posted on <u>June 4, 2011</u> by <u>Chelsea</u>

According to Ralph Keyes, if you aren't scared to write, if you aren't facing demons when you face the blank page (and some call this writer's block), then you may be:

- kidding yourself

- writing banal, inane, trivial stuff

- not writing at all

E.B. White worried over every word. Margaret Atwood said that you need a kind of physical nerve to write, "the kind you need to walk a log across a river." Donald Murray talked about his writing students who had nothing to say on the page, because they felt silence, anxiety, panic, and terror. "Good," he says. "You are at the place from which writing comes."

FIGURE 2.5
Steer clear of ambiguous titles and instead write descriptive titles.

The following samples show unclear and clear titles.

SAMPLE VAGUE TITLES	SAMPLE EXPLANATORY TITLES
Holy Cow!	How to Restring a Guitar
Dashing, Debonair, Delightful Dashes	Recipe for Cranberry Muffins
It's Fantastic	Learn to Say No

Organize for Your Audience

Keep instructions task oriented rather than offering everything you can imagine. Make sure the content is organized for your users' needs, not according to the hierarchy of the organization or your life. Most users don't care about the company's organization.

The sample Web page in **FIGURE 2.6** has an organization that follows the company's interests rather than its readers' interests. The About Us page for any company should focus on the benefits a prospective client receives by hiring the company, not on a hierarchy of who is who within the organization.

About Our Company

The Founders

Jason and Jake Bartholomew founded Web Brothers in 2005, after training for a career in Web Development at Seaside College, in Mayetta Kansas. Jason specialized in Content Management, Jake specialized in graphic design, and so they decided to pool their resources and talents, to bring you the best of all possible worlds in terms of Web design.

Meet the Staff

Jane Allison – Jane is a seasoned Marketing Writer with five years experience creating print and Web content for a multitude of industries.

Carl Thompson – Carl is an artist born in the U.K. He has been painting and drawing since the age of three, and early on decided on a career as a graphic artist.

Bing Freemont – Bing is our Web Sales Wizard. He's part of the reason why Web Brothers has been able to expand! We love Bing.

Our Mission

Our goal at Web Brothers is to provide innovative, quality, well-designed Web sites for small businesses that meet our clients' needs and are cost-effective. We also provide support and maintenance, including security, web hosting, and network support.

What We Can Do for You

Web Brothers offers simple, fresh, and creative Web design, based on your users' needs.

Set the Right Tone

The tone of your story is the atmosphere or mood that it projects. You set the tone with your choice of words, pictures, and sounds. If the tone is serious, you shouldn't use words that convey a silly or trite feeling. If the tone is light-hearted, you shouldn't use images and sounds that are heavy and somber.

Look at the following sample words. Can you see how the workplace terms might be used to convey a work environment that is less fun? Perhaps the author is working in a cubicle, gritting his teeth. The adventure terms set a more optimistic and positive mood, and would be used for a more fun work environment.

WORKPLACE TERMS	ADVENTURE TERMS
Endeavor, slog, work, grind, struggle	Master, achieve, learn, accomplish, realize

Challenges

The best way to get better at writing Web content is to write, write some more, and rewrite. The challenges in this chapter focus on getting to the heart of your topic and deleting needless words.

Freewriting

The freewriting challenges ask you to practice using more active verbs and enhance your observation skills so you can write more precisely.

Freewriting works best when it is timed. If you tend to write quickly, set the timer for ten minutes. If you tend to take a little more time, give yourself 15 minutes. Remember that with freewriting you don't need to worry about accuracy, grammar, spelling, and so forth.

GOT HAS GOT TO GO

Rewrite the following scenario, replacing all forms of the verb *got* with active, specific verbs.

> When I got to my car, I tried to get the door open, but my key got stuck in the lock. "Oh, I get it," I said to myself. I had gotten to the wrong car. I got more than a little worried that I wouldn't get to my next appointment on time, which would get me in the doghouse with my boss. I got a hold of the key and twisted, but it got jammed even more, and then it got broken off. I got sweaty even thinking about how late it was getting. I got my phone out and got in touch with the security guard, Mr. Jarvis. When he got to the car and got an understanding of the problem, he said, "I'm afraid we've got to call a locksmith to get this thing resolved." He sighed, getting his knees all dirty as he got down to get a good look at the key that had gotten stuck in the lock. "Could you get in touch with the owner of this car, Mr. Jarvis," I pleaded. "I've got to go. If I get to my next appointment much later than I already am I'll get in hot water with the boss." Mr. Jarvis got a frown on his face, and then he said, "OK." I was so glad that I had gotten into the habit of keeping an extra key at my desk. I got to my desk. I got out the extra key. I got to my car and got a good look at it before I tried to get the door open. I got the engine started and got on my way. Pretty soon I got to the freeway and boy, did I ever get excited to see that there was no traffic. But soon I got going a little too fast. Then I got pulled over by the CHP. I got a ticket.

OBSERVE WITH NEW EYES

Good writing begins with keen observation. For this exercise, pretend that you have just landed on the planet and are seeing everything in your backyard for the very first time. Take a walk outside with your notebook. Keep your eyes wide open. Find something new, something you've never before noticed. You might find a plant that's thriving or one that's barely surviving; you might watch someone favoring one leg while walking. Perhaps you'll see a child poking a caterpillar, hear an odd noise, or smell exhaust on the street. Maybe you'll see a strange car or hear a cricket that sounds like it smoked Camels all its life.

Make notes of all of your observations. You might also sketch what you see. Then find a quiet place to write. Write three paragraphs about what you observed.

Suggested Exercises

Exercises are longer projects that will take more time to complete. You can find more complete instructions, learning outcomes, and criteria for critiquing your work at www.write4web.com.

REVISE YOUR FAVORITE AUTHOR'S SENTENCES

Find a sentence, either online or in print, written by your favorite author. Every writer can improve. Take that sentence and revise it so it follows the best practices from the Web.

Here's a sentence Faulkner wrote in *The Sound and the Fury* that could use your help:

> "With the sun and all in my eyes and my blood going so I kept thinking every time my head would go on and burst and get it over with, with briers and things grabbing at me, then I came into the sand ditch where they had been and I recognized the tree where the car was, and just as I got out of the ditch and started running I heard the car start."

Up Next

With the best practices of good writing under your belt, you can now move on and decide how to complement your writing with visuals. Chapter 3, "Working with Images," provides guidance to ensure that your images add to rather than detract from the story you are telling. Finding the right tool for the story, whether it's an illustration, a graph, a photo, or a painting, is an important aspect of good writing.

3

Working with Images

As the saying goes, *a picture is worth a thousand words*. But what do those thousand words express? They might convey a clear story or perhaps just mumbo jumbo—a visual mishmash that doesn't fit the story. The picture could be incomprehensible. Or it could have a complicated meaning that, without a few words of text, takes too long to grasp. Although the visual might be worth a thousand words, the message you want to communicate might only be worth ten words.

This chapter discusses different types of images you might consider for your Web content and offers suggestions to make sure your images add to rather than detract from the story. Read this chapter to understand how to:

- Choose the right type of image
- Make sure the image is clear and easy to understand
- Make sure your images tell stories
- Make sure your images don't irritate the reader

Choose the Right Type of Image

Choosing the right type of image is as important as getting the image right. You have so many choices! For example, your options include line art, clip art, photography, charts, tables, word art, and so forth. With line art alone, you have several choices. You could use a simple computer-generated illustration that has a basic two-dimensional look, a shaded and fully rendered illustration that appears three dimensional, or even a scanned etching or drawing. With photography, you might choose a shot that shows an object in clear focus, or you might choose a mood shot that has a more ethereal look. The possibilities are abundant!

With so many prospects, how do you know which is the most effective type of image to use? The following list briefly describes a few types of images and how you might best use each:

- **Clip art.** Shows simple, more generic images. Clip art is typically low-resolution and looks painted rather than drawn. Often, clip art is a simple, black image on a white background. (Most illustration packages come bundled with ready-made clip art.) Clip art works fine for borders and backgrounds, but in general, use it sparingly or not at all. When your readers see clip art, they can easily get the impression that the content is not serious, professional, or valuable.

- **Line art.** Uses distinct lines, straight and curved, to depict an image. With computer-generated line art, the lines are formed mathematically and called vectors. You can easily resize the art without concern that the image will become blurred. Line art works well to illustrate product instructions and technical information, because the art is clean and easy to read, and because you can enlarge it without the image becoming pixelated.

- **Photography.** Records real-life objects and scenes. Photos work well for most Web content and can show exact items, comparisons, mood, point of view, and so on. For technical instructions, photos can be harder to interpret than line drawings, graphs, and tables.

- **Paintings.** Provide either a realistic or interpretive image. Paintings work well to convey a mood or set the tone of your story.

- **Tables, graphs, and charts.** Help readers quickly visualize and understand data. Tables especially work well when you want the reader to compare two or more items. Your readers are familiar with line, bar, and pie charts because they are commonly used in magazines and newspapers. Pie charts work well to show percentages; line and bar charts work well to show trends.

- **Word art.** Provides interest and visual appeal to a story. Word art can also help break up long sections of text.

Why would you choose one type of image over another? The image you choose needs to fit the story, fit your readers' expectations, and send the right message. Another important consideration is the cost of the image, not only in terms of money, but also in terms of effort and time.

Send the Right Message

For any image that you use, you should determine what message the image conveys. What is the main story that you are telling, and how does that image contribute to the story?

Sometimes your reasons to choose one type of image over another are obvious. You know exactly what response you want from your readers, so you can find or create the exact image that will elicit that response. Let's say, for example, that you want to sell a guitar on eBay. You want to show the guitar in your eBay ad in a way that sends the following messages to potential bidders:

- The guitar is worth buying. It looks good and will play well.
- The seller is honest and credible and will ship the guitar promptly and carefully after the sale.
- This very moment is the right time to bid on this guitar.

When you're selling an item on the Web, you want to represent that item exactly as it looks, and you want it to look good. For the guitar, it's an easy choice to take a snapshot (**FIGURE 3.1**) or two to show the entire guitar, front and back. But because you want the guitar to look good, you'll make sure that the lighting is good when you take the photo.

FIGURE 3.1
Represent an item for sale as it looks, only better.

Great art picks up where nature ends.

—Marc Chagall

It might be tempting to show a mood shot (**FIGURE 3.2**) of the guitar to make potential buyers feel the guitar will bring some sort of magic to their lives. However, because you are advertising the guitar on eBay, you know the reader is likely to be wary and suspicious of an image that does not show the guitar in full focus.

FIGURE 3.2
Mood shot of the guitar.

You would not choose clip art (**FIGURE 3.3**) to represent the guitar. Clip art has a cartoonish feel, and with it the reader will not get the messages you want to convey. The reader might think you have a toy guitar, or that you aren't a credible seller. Or maybe you don't even have a guitar.

Although a drawing or painting of the guitar might look beautiful, these types of images are also not a good choice for eBay. Line art would work well if you were writing an instructional story and wanted to show your reader how to restring the guitar. But when you want the reader to buy the guitar, you want to show an accurate picture of the exact guitar you are selling. Otherwise, the reader won't feel warm and fuzzy about buying it.

After deciding the type of image that best fits your story, you'll need to assess your budget, how much time you have, and whether you'll create the art yourself or acquire it.

FIGURE 3.3
Clip art of the guitar.

Finding Affordable Art

Writing for the Web can be overwhelming if you feel you have to do everything by yourself. It's wonderful to have the capability to add breathtaking, colorful imagery to your stories, but you might not currently have the skill set, desire, or time to produce the graphic that best fits the story. Fortunately, it's not difficult to acquire affordable, professional, and royalty-free art. Here are a few suggestions:

- Find stock art that fits the story and your budget.
- Partner with a colleague or friend and share talents.
- Purchase art from a professional artist.

Every image in your Web content should have the three characteristics discussed in Chapter 1: clarity, spark, and meaning. The next section offers guidelines to make sure your images are clear and meaningful.

Google *stock art* and choose a site that offers stock imagery. Then browse through the different categories available. For example, look for *abstract* photos. Start a list of types of images and write down what you like and don't like about each type.

Keep the Message Clear

You've most likely had the experience of viewing a picture on the Web or on TV and saying, "What the heck?" because it doesn't make sense or doesn't fit the context of the story. Ideally, your readers will be so involved in the story that they won't think about the images at all. But if the image is confusing, it's guaranteed to slow down readers or lose them.

Don't Clutter Your Images

Just as you don't want extra verbiage to clutter your sentences and paragraphs, you don't want extra details to clutter your images. In fact, because imagery grabs your readers' attention more than words, it's even more important to keep your images streamlined and clutter free. When you're revising, make one pass just to make sure every image fits with the paragraph or chunk that refers to it. Then make another pass to see if any images can be cleaned up or simplified.

Go to one of your favorite Web sites and scrutinize every image. Does it add to the story? Does it detract from the story? Does it fit? Is it a clean image without extra details? Jot down your critique of the images overall. Then make notes of any images that could be simplified.

Use Plenty of White Space

Use white space liberally; the empty space feels restful, whereas art without any white space feels wild and frenetic. You don't need to cram minutiae into every pixel (**FIGURE 3.4**). Frame the important details in the image with plenty of blank space. For your readers, sorting through images crammed with detail is too much work.

FIGURE 3.4

A crowded image.

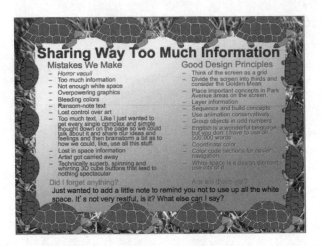

FIGURE 3.4

A crowded image.

JUST SAY NO TO *HORROR VACUI*

The Latin phrase *horror vacui* means fear of empty space. It's used by critics to describe art where the entire surface or art board is crammed with details. Ancient Egyptian art, where a repetition of symbols and patterns fills in every blank spot, is said to have *horror vacui*. Various cultures through the ages have shown an affinity for a more elaborate style where every nook and cranny is filled. Compare the complicated style of Victorian drawing rooms with the sleek style of living rooms in the 1950s. Your Web readers, typically, will appreciate the sleek, spare style.

Don't Use Confusing Elements

It's easy to add a confusing element to an image by getting sidetracked, by attempting to show too much, or by accident. Ask yourself what the main message or take-away message is for an image. Is that message clearly in the image? Your images should feel like billboards to readers. Readers should be able to take in the content while speeding past the image at 65 miles per hour.

Does the image have a mixed message? For example, you might be attempting to show an economic downturn, yet someone in the crowd is making a call on an expensive smart phone. Is there something odd about the image that draws the reader's attention? With photos, a common mistake is to take a shot without paying attention to the background. For example, you might have a shot of a woman with an electrical tower in the background. In the photo, it looks like the tower is growing out of the woman's head, like she has some sort of odd antenna.

Just as with language, images can also have unintentional mixed metaphors. If the background of a graphic shows clouds and there are links in the foreground depicted as starfish, you've mixed up the sky and the sea.

Avoid Death by PowerPoint

You and your readers probably loathe PowerPoint presentations, which are famous for putting people to sleep. Here are a few of the unlikeable qualities about PowerPoint slide shows that are unappealing in any Web images that appear as slides:

- Repetition of the same elements causes eye fatigue. Although pictures, tables, and graphs should have a consistent style, make sure your readers don't feel like they are driving at night and your images have formed the white line between lanes, hypnotizing them into falling asleep.

- Reducing complex thoughts or processes into simple elements, such as bullet points, that tell only partial stories. You want concise, clean images, but you don't want to distill all the meaning out of them.

- Offset images that appear to wobble from page to page. If you are showing a series of similar objects, place them consistently in the same location on the page so the image doesn't jump from page to page.

We are all hungry and thirsty for concrete images. Abstract art will have been good for one thing: to restore its exact virginity to figurative art.

—Salvador Dali

Add Words Wherever Helpful

For Web pages, words are typically the glue that holds all the media together to shape the story. For images, a short, clear phrase can also help convey the message the image portrays. Make sure you explain images well with captions, callouts, titles, and explanatory text where appropriate. For example, if you want to show that an item is easy to carry and fits nicely in a pocket, the few words "Fits in your pocket" get the point across quickly.

Don't Irritate Your Viewers

There's nothing more frustrating for your readers than landing on a page that suddenly turns the cursor into sparkles or has startling rollover buttons that jump up and down. Here are a few common problems that will just annoy your readers:

- Fuzzy, pixelated graphics.
- Graphics that are sized too small or too large. If the art looks like a postage stamp, your readers will bypass it. If it's too large, your readers will feel like they have to take a step backwards to take it in. It can also look childish and unprofessional.

- Graphics that allow the reader to size them up or down, but when the reader chooses this option, the graphics display at the same size that originally appeared.
- Jittery animations, flash, abrasive rollovers, and sparkly cursors.
- Text with bleeding colors.
- Callouts with teeny fonts (less than 9 points).
- Nonuniform line weights or colors.

Telling a Story

Telling stories is an inherent part of the human experience. Your readers love stories! With images, readers can become instantly and effortlessly involved in the story.

Once you have determined the story you want to tell and know what message you want the reader to take away, you'll need to plan how you'll use images to tell the story. Let's look at a few ideas.

Showing a Process

Although one image can work to show a process, more often it's easier for your readers to understand the process with a few images.

The set of photos in **FIGURE 3.5** shows the simple process of boiling water.

FIGURE 3.5
Show a process: boiling water.

For technical writing, line art often works better than photography when you're explaining a procedure, such as how to change batteries in a device. Compare **FIGURE 3.6** to **FIGURE 3.7**. In the photo, the lines of the device are hard to see. The line art (Figure 3.7) more clearly shows where the batteries are located.

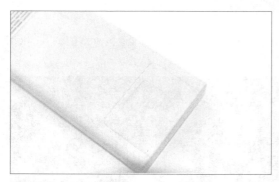

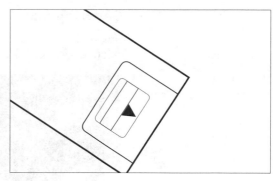

FIGURE 3.6
A photo can be blurry when you're providing instructions.

FIGURE 3.7
Line art works best for technical instruction.

Showing a Concept

Concepts, by definition, are abstract and therefore more difficult to share. Using an image to portray a concept helps readers understand the idea or thought and can also deepen the experience.

The photo in **FIGURE 3.8** displays the figurative notion of a romantic evening with a concrete image.

FIGURE 3.8
Show a concept:
a romantic evening.

Setting the Mood or Tone

Images, more than text, set the mood and tone of your Web story. Think of mood as the feelings your readers have while they are viewing the story, such as joy, happiness, anger, fear, suspicion, or hatred. Think of tone as the attitude of the story itself, such as ironic, sarcastic, pessimistic, optimistic, or benevolent.

The photo of the guitar in Figure 3.2 might evoke a positive mood, like hope or contentedness. The tone might be playful or romantic.

Showing Size

Images are fantastic for giving your readers a sense of big or small, tall or short (FIGURE 3.9).

FIGURE 3.9
A picture showing scale.

Use pictures to help your readers get their heads around hard-to-imagine sizes and numbers. Let's say, for example, you want your readers to get a sense of the grandness of the Grand Canyon. Rather than telling readers how many acres or miles the Grand Canyon covers, it would be better to show it off with a magnificent landscape photo. If you place a person in the foreground of the photo and show the Grand Canyon in the background, the viewer has a sense of scale as well.

Think of the Global Audience

While choosing graphics, remember that your readers can come from all cultures and all walks of life. Choose pictures of people that aren't limited by age, gender, culture, or skin color.

Make your images accessible to those with challenges, such as people with low vision or color blindness, or those who only know English as a second language.

You'll want to reach the largest audience possible. Let's look at a few ways to avoid images that appear provincial.

Add Diversity

In your pictures, show people of all sizes, ages, colors, and so forth. Make sure your images don't depict everyone as homogeneous (**FIGURE 3.10**).

FIGURE 3.10
Show diversity.

Avoid Colloquialisms

Avoid images that look too provincial or colloquial for the story you are telling. Make sure people in the images don't appear as stereotypes.

Make Sure Humor Translates

Humor often does not translate well across cultures. Jokes typically make fun of someone or some situation. When you attempt humor, you risk offending a reader. At the very least, a reader might feel that you are insensitive. If you want to add humor, test it out on several individuals who are in your audience. If there's any doubt, leave it out.

Isn't life a series of images that change as they repeat themselves?

—Andy Warhol

Avoid Embedded Text in a Graphic

Embedding text in an image (**FIGURE 3.11**) is almost always a bad idea for the following reasons:

- The text makes the image look cluttered.
- If the content needs to be translated to another language, the text will not get translated.

- Any revisions to the text are more difficult to make than if the text is outside of the image.
- The text is not accessible and won't be translated to speech for viewers who use readers.

FIGURE 3.11
Image with embedded text.

Eat six to nine
servings of
fruits and
vegetables
per day

Make Images Accessible

Viewers who have challenges, such as low vision, use a screen reader to understand Web content. The screen reader uses software to convert text to speech or to output the text on a Braille printer.

To make images accessible and to allow the screen reader to convey what the image means, you need to add a descriptive label to the image, which is typically called ALT TEXT. When you write the descriptive label, make certain that you carefully express what the image conveys.

To learn more about making your Web content accessible, visit the Web Accessibility Initiative (WAI) at www.w3.org/WAI.

Using Tables, Charts, and Graphs

Tables, charts, and graphs help your reader *see* data and quickly understand it. It takes a little more time on your part to analyze the data and decide what type of table or chart will work best. Familiarity helps, so keep in mind that your readers have already seen plenty of pie and bar charts, line graphs, and tables. However, your audience might not be as familiar with scatterplots or bubble charts.

Here are a few guidelines for composing tables, charts, and graphs:

- **Standardize formats.** You don't want the work to look like you couldn't make up your mind on a style or as if there were several authors. Keep line weights consistent for tables. Choose colors that will work for all the graphs and tables. Limit fonts, and use the same font and font size for callouts, table heads, and so on.

- **Consistently place tables and graphs on a page.** Keep the margins uniform. If the reader moves through slides, place tables and graphs in the same location, so they don't appear to wobble or float around. If the tables have similar columns, keep the columns in the same place and at the same widths.

- **Avoid using lots of text.** As with most Web content, use as little text as possible. With slides, a good rule of thumb is to have less than 40 words per page.

Challenges

The best way to get better at writing Web content is to write, write some more, and rewrite. The challenges in this chapter focus on working with images.

Freewriting

The freewriting challenge in this chapter asks you to practice writing with an image in mind. Freewriting works best when it is timed. If you tend to write quickly, set the timer for ten minutes. If you tend to take a little more time, give yourself 15 minutes. Remember that with freewriting you don't need to worry about accuracy, grammar, spelling, and so forth.

I FEEL NAKED WITHOUT IT

What is it that you can't leave home without? What do you feel lost without? Write about something that you have to have with you at all times or you're uncomfortable.

Suggested Exercise

Exercises are longer projects that will take more time to complete. You can find more complete instructions, learning outcomes, and criteria for critiquing your work at www.write4web.com.

PHOTO STORY

Tell a story with one photo and words. The objective is to tell your story seamlessly, integrating the image with your words. The image should carry some of the weight of the narrative. In other words, the photo tells part of the story, and without it, the story would not be complete.

For the photo, choose any image that works well with your story idea.

Here are a few ideas for your topic:

- A person you know well
- Someone you don't know but admire
- A place that makes you feel happy or threatened
- An event that was exciting
- Activities that bother you
- A sport that you enjoy
- Your pet

Up Next

Now that you've thought about still images and what works and what to avoid, you can move on to consider adding moving graphics to your Web content. Chapter 4, "Adding Motion," provides guidelines for adding video, animation, or any other type of moving image to your Web stories.

4

Adding Motion

There's no question about it: Moving images dazzle and mesmerize. Cinema has been around for over 100 years, and audiences are still willing to sit in dark rooms among strangers to watch the big screen. Video, even on the teeny screen of a mobile device, can hypnotize viewers. There is magic in telling stories with visuals in motion. If you get it right, there's no better way to draw in your readers and keep their attention.

This chapter examines the various media you might choose to show graphics in motion, such as video, animation, photo slide shows, and simulations. It also provides an overview and explains the ways to get started with adding moving images to your Web content. The topics in this chapter include:

- Deciding to use graphics in motion
- Brainstorming
- Developing a storyboard
- Writing scripts
- Using guidelines to produce video and animation

If you find your passions ignited about animation, video, educational technology, and so on, and you want to deepen your knowledge, see www.write4web.com for a list of schools, Web sites, and books.

Getting Started with Motion

The good news about designing content for the Web is that you're not limited to one media or another. You can incorporate video, animation, photo slide shows, illustrations, text, music, audio narration, and so on. You just have to make sure your story meets your readers' expectations and needs. Think of your reader as Goldilocks. The story should be *just right* in terms of timing, pacing, style, length, and complexity. Plus it needs to have clarity, spark, and meaning.

Deciding to Use Moving Graphics

The first question you need to ask yourself is whether or not it's a good idea to add moving graphics or animated text to your Web story. You don't want to annoy the reader with gratuitous noise or motion, but there are definite cases in which moving pictures can get readers excited, show a message, or instruct much better than text, still images, or sound.

Your decision to incorporate moving graphics into your story might be easier when you know the types of moving graphics available to you and how to use them successfully.

Types of Moving Graphics

Technology, design, and computer terminology are in a constant state of flux, which blurs the lines between the different types of media. Nonetheless, the following list attempts to briefly describe some types of moving graphics and how you might best use each:

- **Video** shows real-life, moving images, instantly immersing readers in place and time. Video is perfect for promoting products and messages, capturing personal histories, presenting interviews, and providing instructions.

- **Animation** takes individual pictures of characters or objects and shows them in continuous movement. The kid in all of us loves cartoons. Animations work well for short ads, product demos, Web introductions, and games. For instructions on complicated activities, such as tying knots, dance steps, or juggling, animation works best.

- **Motion graphics** are created by designers who work with software applications to make three-dimensional logos spin across the screen, film titles dance and weave, and images fly across the screen and then evaporate.

- **Software simulation** models the experience of using a software program by showing the software screens and mouse movements for typical tasks. Simulation is ideal for promoting software packages and for instruction on tools within the software application. For example, simulation works well if you need to show readers how to use the Bezier Pen tool in a design application.

Also, the simulation needs to be paced just right. If it's too slow, readers will get distracted. If it's too fast, readers will get frustrated.

- **Games** provide entertainment and can be educational. Make sure your audience thinks the game is as fun as you do. As with all Web content, your audience is key. Games for the corporate environment are nothing like games you play at home.

- **Photo slide shows** show people best. Still pictures can provide a more emotional experience than video, especially when combined with Burns effects (panning across the image and zooming in or out).

- **Digital storytelling** works well for personal stories and educational purposes. You can find wonderful examples and more information at www.storycenter.org.

700 BILLION YOUTUBE VIDEOS

It's only recent advances in technologies that have given you the capability to easily add animation and video to your Web content. And readers are wild about it! YouTube.com was registered in 2005. Just five years later, YouTube (youtube-global.blogspot.com) announced, "During 2010, you all watched more than 700 billion YouTube videos and uploaded more than 13 million hours of video."

But before you can narrow down the type of media you'll use, you'll need to come up with an idea to set in motion. Brainstorming is an excellent way to unearth ideas, and writing down your ideas can help you flesh them out.

Capturing an Idea for Video or Animation

Where do you get your ideas? That's a question all authors are asked and asked often. It can be a difficult question to answer, because ideas can come from anywhere and anything. The more you think and talk about an idea, the more it morphs into something else. You're driving in your car, listening to a favorite radio station and boom! A fantastic idea hits you. Or you're talking with a friend and suddenly you stop listening, because something wonderful is percolating in your head. You don't want to be rude, so you share that idea with your friend. The friend catches on and takes the idea a step in another direction. In a heartbeat, you're collaborating. It's a fascinating process when you're just letting the thoughts gallop around in your head. However, trying to tie down ideas for a creative project can be exasperating.

Ever tried. Ever failed. No matter. Try Again. Fail again. Fail better.

—Samuel Beckett

Just for fun, try capturing
your ideas for a story
on napkins, the backs of
envelopes, the palm of
your hand if you don't mind
a temporary tattoo, paper
bags, the backs of receipts,
the blank side of a greeting
card, or any scrap of paper
you have handy. It's good
to be flexible.

You are the only one who knows what works best to capture an idea and begin the design process. But here are some ideas for brainstorming that have worked well for others:

- **Sticky notes.** Jot down anything and everything that comes to mind on sticky notes (**FIGURE 4.1**). Place the notes on a large surface, such as a wall or tabletop. Move the notes around as you continue to add notes.

- **3 x 5 cards.** Index cards work the same as sticky notes but give you the added flexibility of designing on the go. Keep them in your back pocket while you're out taking a walk.

- **Lists.** Make lists of whatever you think of that relates to one or more ideas.

- **An outline.** If you like working with outlines, this is probably the best way for you to begin.

- **Napkins.** Seriously, napkins work as well as sticky notes and can be fun for collaborations.

When you finally have an idea that's nearly hatched, you can begin developing it along a timeline. That's where a storyboard helps.

FIGURE 4.1
Use sticky notes to collect
and sort ideas.

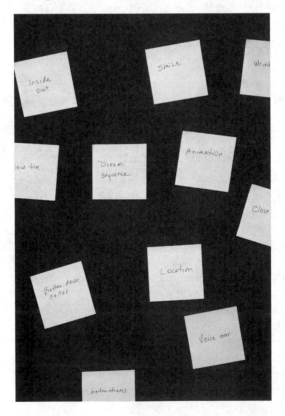

Developing the Story

Whether your work is fiction or nonfiction, it has to tell a good story. For video and animation, it's especially important to plan the story. You need to understand the concept, the structure, the setting, the action, any spoken narration, and so forth. You need to determine how all the multimedia elements will work together. The time spent planning is time well spent. If you've ever worked on a complex project that used seat-of-the-pants planning, you understand the trouble and frustration you can encounter that can easily be prevented by thinking through the design, developing a storyboard, and discussing with any team members or stakeholders what the final production will look like.

If we are to change our world view, images have to change.

—Vaclav Havel

The first important step in your planning is to develop a storyboard.

Designing a Storyboard

Storyboards are design tools that show the main action on the screen over time. A storyboard also lists all the media for each scene, such as sound effects, voice-over, music, and text, and describes how they all work together. Not only does the storyboard gather all the ideas on paper with a timeline, but it is also conducive for generating and building additional ideas. Designing a storyboard provides a few more benefits as well, because it:

- **Records the plan.** It documents the creative process by placing a stake in the ground for the initial starting point. From there you can use it to track changes.

- **Persuades stakeholders.** If you need to persuade someone else to pay for the production, a storyboard helps whoever holds the purse strings to make a good decision. It helps you convince someone that the production will be worth the cost.

- **Informs team members.** If you're working with a team of artists, writers, and programmers, the storyboard keeps everyone in line. You can use the storyboard as a reference for developing schedules and assigning responsibilities.

- **Establishes a blueprint.** A storyboard keeps you from making costly mistakes during production, because it provides you with a clear plan. The tailor's maxim is to measure twice, cut once. Completing a storyboard is like measuring twice.

- **Creates a working agreement.** If you're working with a client or a boss, the storyboard educates that person, documents agreements, and keeps the process moving. It's completely frustrating to be halfway through a project and hear the client say, for the first time, "Oh, we need to..." With a storyboard in place, you can gently remind the boss or client that you are following the original direction and any changes at this stage will cost more and take more time.

The format for the storyboard depends on the people you are working with and their expectations. Every storyboard needs a brief introduction to describe the work's main idea or message. In addition, every storyboard needs to state the targeted audience and the objectives or goals for the work.

For the corporate environment, it's likely that you'll need to set the expectations. If you're working on a training demonstration for instance, you might use a simple, three-column format (**FIGURE 4.2**).

FIGURE 4.2
A three-column storyboard format.

Storyboard		
Title		
Producer (Your Name)		
Artists (Photos)		
Composers (Music)		
Speakers		
Visuals	**Audio**	**Production Notes**
Add video, animation, still images, and text here.	Add narration, music, and sound effects here.	Add production notes here.

If you're collaborating with a team in the corporate environment, PowerPoint works fine as a storyboard tool. Place the visuals in the slide view, and then add all the information about other media in the speaker's notes.

For animation, storyboards are typically a series of framed, hand-drawn scenes. If you're not a fine artist or you don't like to draw, don't be alarmed. Stick figures work fine. If you feel self-conscious about your stick figures, draw balloons around their legs and arms to fill them out. Make sure, in the storyboard, that you change the perspective for scenes, showing them as wide or long shots (from a distance), mid-range, and close up (**FIGURE 4.3**).

FIGURE 4.3
A storyboard for animation.

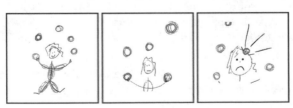

Rapid Prototyping

Another way to design a digital production is to use a method called *rapid prototyping*. With rapid prototyping, you need to work with design tools to rapidly create a prototype of the final production. This works especially well with productions that can take weeks to develop, such as computer-based training.

Using rapid prototyping, you need to set expectations and let those who will be reviewing the prototype know that it is only the beginning of development and design. You can call the prototype a "quick-and-dirty" version of the final production. You want it to have imperfections at this point for a number of reasons:

- **Preliminary design feedback.** You want the prototype to be a design tool rather than the finished product. If it's too perfect, the reviewer or client might have a look and say, "Great! Let me have it. Send me the bill." Although pleasing the reviewer is satisfying, at this stage you're better off getting reviewers to offer suggestions and describe likes and dislikes.

- **Big picture critique.** You don't want to focus on minute details, such as the choice of fonts or color at this stage. Set expectations and tell reviewers and collaborators that the prototype is in its infancy, and it's not the time to spend hours crossing Ts and dotting Is. You definitely don't want to spend days searching for just the right shade of mango that your boss has in mind.

- **Team/client participation.** You want others to feel that they have taken an active part in the production, not just accepted your final product. Consider all suggestions carefully. But also remember that *you* are the author, and the final production will represent *your* work. Don't simply roll over and say yes to all suggestions that come your way.

For more information about storytelling methods, read Chapter 9, "Telling a Good Story."

Whichever storytelling approach you use, a good and simple way to structure your Web story is with three major parts.

Adding an Introduction, Body, and Close

According to Aristotle, a story needs a beginning, middle, and end, and your story with moving images is no exception.

For video blogs (also called vlogs), the introduction can be the title page and the ending can be the credits. If you're planning a series of videos, you'll want to give all the introductions and endings a similar look and feel, so your readers will recognize the series.

The middle of the video should tell the story. If you're not sure how to construct the middle, try following this simple organization:

1. Show the overview. Show a long camera shot as the audio narration speaks the introduction (**FIGURE 4.4**).

2. Show a mid-range shot as audio narration gives more specifics about the story (**FIGURE 4.5**).

3 Show a close-up shot and describe details with the audio narration (**FIGURE 4.6**).

try this

Imagine that you are showing a production to someone important, like the VP of marketing where you work. You've worked night and day on the production and feel certain it's going to wow the VP. Sadly, you don't get the response you're expecting. The VP does the equivalent of crumpling up a piece of paper, sneers, and says the entire thing is sophomoric and distasteful. Take a deep breath. How will you respond? Make a list of your thoughts.

FIGURE 4.4
Provide a long shot to start the story.

FIGURE 4.5
Provide a mid-range shot to continue the story.

FIGURE 4.6
A close-up of details to go deeper into the story.

The Animation or Video Setting

The setting is a combination of the location and the time. For example, the story might occur in the 1950s in Paris. Setting is important. For theater scripts, AT RISE appears at the beginning, and it tells what the audience sees when the curtain rises for the first scene. What does your audience see AT RISE for your first scene?

Make sure the setting meets the audience's expectations. For instance, if your story is about skydiving, the audience expects to see the sky, an airport, or the inside of an airplane. See Chapter 1 for more information on understanding your audience.

For video, remember that the camera can see more than you typically do. For example, if you're producing a video that shows how to make an exotic dish, make sure your kitchen is spotless and there aren't any crumbs on the counter.

Writing Scripts for Video and Animation

A written script provides a road map for your production and example dialogue for any spoken words in your story. It can also briefly explain the setting, action, lighting, and transitions. If you are the author, the director, the editor, and the producer, you don't need as many details. But if you are handing off the script to someone else to direct and produce, you'll want to add more detail.

You might think you can't write a script without screenwriting software. Shakespeare did not have a software application to help him write *The Tempest*, and it turned out pretty well. You don't need a screenwriting program to write a good script.

You might think you don't really need a script, but there are several good reasons to have one:

- When recording voice-overs or for any spoken narration that accompanies the visuals, a script helps you and other speakers remember what to say and when to say it.
- A script prevents some ahs, ers, and ums that would need to be edited out.
- A script stops some spontaneous, impromptu nonsense that would need to be eliminated.
- A script briefly describes settings for scenes.
- A script briefly describes action during a scene. Is the main character pulling out her hair when she says, "No, I don't want to," or is she stamping her foot?
- A script provides a minimal amount of stage direction.

The format you use for writing a script should be clean and easy to read, but there are no strict rules unless you are writing a screenplay and are hoping to sell it. Scripts don't use quotation marks around dialogue, and characters are shown in ALL CAPs.

For more details about writing dialogue, read Chapter 5, "Adding Sound."

FIGURE 4.7 shows a short sample script.

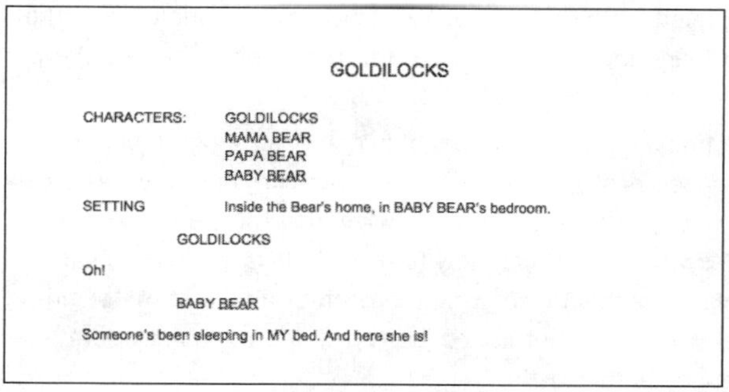

GOLDILOCKS

CHARACTERS: GOLDILOCKS
MAMA BEAR
PAPA BEAR
BABY BEAR

SETTING Inside the Bear's home, in BABY BEAR's bedroom.

GOLDILOCKS

Oh!

BABY BEAR

Someone's been sleeping in MY bed. And here she is!

FIGURE 4.7
A sample script.

Guidelines for Video and Animation

Designers tend to make several common mistakes when they produce animation or video. Here are a few problems you can easily avoid when you make your own productions:

- **Talking heads.** Your video is an interview of one or two people, and the footage simply shows one face and then another. You can fix this by adding more interesting visuals while the speakers are talking. But do you even need visuals? If the audio story is arresting, think about simply producing an audio podcast of the interview and leaving out the video footage altogether.

- **Panning and zooming too quickly.** Use a tripod and don't let the camera person drink too much coffee. Tailor the speed of the panning to the audience, but keep in mind that members of the audience don't want to feel like they're on a rollercoaster ride.

- **Little or no sound.** Even the silent films, before talkies, had a pianist or organ player to accompany the movie. Without any sound at all, your images can feel empty. If the video shows someone making something, either have the person talk the viewer through the process or add voice-over. A podcast without visuals works fine, but most video or animation needs sound.

- **Timing is too slow or too fast.** For photo slide shows, three seconds per slide works well unless there is a lengthy pan or zoom. Seconds add up. If the scenes fly by too quickly, the audience feels cheated.

- **Not providing a way to print out detailed information.** If you're showing complicated mixes or technical instructions, you'll want to also give the reader an opportunity to print out the information. For example, if you've produced a video on how to make samosas, also provide the recipe, in text, for the reader.

- **No transitions.** Transitions help connect scenes, keep the audience on the same train of thought, and offer resting spots during the production. A simple, common transition is simply to cut to the next scene.

- **Too many scenes.** Modern audiences are quick to move from one scene to the next and don't need all the intermediary scenes that an audience in the 1970s needed. Compare any TV sitcom from the 1960s with a recent show, and you'll see the difference.

- **Impersonal instructions.** When a real person is demonstrating an action, such as folding a paper airplane, and only the hands are shown, viewers can feel as if they are watching a robot. Also, showing only mouse movements and screen captures when explaining how to use a software program can distance your viewers. Fix this by showing a person or a face at the beginning of the story and when you introduce the topic, and by making sure any audio narration sounds enthusiastic.

Here are a few suggestions to consider while producing the visual work:

- Keep it short.
- Keep it simple. Don't try to include more than one idea.
- Keep your audience in mind.
- Keep the lighting suitable for any camera work.
- Keep it fun.

For a good example of an engaging, interactive video online, watch *The Test Tube* with David Suzuki at http://testtube.nfb.ca. The first thing you'll see is a question for you to respond to: "If you could find an extra minute right now, what would you do?" After you type in your answer, the show begins. Your response connects with real-time Twitter updates from around the world on the same topic.

Challenges

The best way to get better at writing Web content is to write, write some more, and rewrite. The challenges in this chapter focus on working with moving images.

Freewriting

The freewriting challenge in this chapter asks you to practice writing a script with an image in mind.

Freewriting works best when it is timed. If you tend to write quickly, set the timer for ten minutes. If you tend to take a little more time, give yourself 15 minutes. Remember that with freewriting you don't need to worry about accuracy, grammar, spelling, and so forth.

AFTER 43 YEARS, BARBIE AND KEN SPLIT UP

Early in 2003, Mattel announced that it was indeed time for the plastic couple to spend some time apart (**FIGURE 4.8**).

FIGURE 4.8
Barbie and Ken's last date.

Imagine that Barbie and Ken are on a double date with Midge and G.I. Joe (Barbie's best friend and Ken's best friend). It's the day before they decide to call it quits. The setting is a bar with a dance floor. Choose another setting if you like.

- What are the four characters saying?
- What are they wearing?
- What is the action?
- Describe the setting.

Suggested Exercise

Exercises are longer projects that will take more time to complete. You can find more complete instructions, learning outcomes, and criteria for critiquing your work at www.write4web.com.

STORYBOARDING

Using stick figures, create the storyboard for instructions on how to tie a tie or a silk scarf. Make sure you include:

- An introduction
- A description of the target audience
- A description of the media you will use
- Wide shots, mid-range shots, and close-ups
- An ending

Decide whether you will use animation or video to produce the instructions.

When you are finished, search the Web to find many examples of instructions for both tying a tie and tying a scarf. For examples of both animated instructions and video, see www.tie-a-tie.net. How would your production be better?

Up Next

Now that you've learned about moving graphics and realized how they might enhance your Web content, you can continue on and read about adding sound. Chapter 5, "Adding Sound," explores the dimensions of sound and how human voice affects a story.

5

Adding Sound

You've been developing your sensibilities for sound for longer than you can remember. Before you were born, you listened to your mother's heartbeat. As your mother's heartbeat quickened or slowed, you began to understand rhythm, beat, pitch, loudness, and softness. Whatever sounds your mother liked and disliked she shared with you. If she listened to classical music, you felt the slow, soothing or high and frenetic vibrations pass through your mother's body. If she sighed, you heard that, too. You heard the rush of air when she took a sharp breath. Maybe your mother sang lullabies to you while you were in the crib. Maybe you had an aunt who liked to rap. Maybe your father had a muscle car that he loved to tinker with, and somewhere in your brain is that memory, the sound of your father's tools clinking against metal, the sound of that car sputtering and growling.

All the sounds that you've listened to all these years have developed your *ear*. Now, as you're contemplating adding sound to your Web content, you already know what you find pleasing or jarring. While you're reading this chapter, reflect on your preferences for sound and think about what might work for your audience. This chapter covers:

- Choosing sound for Web content
- Adding sound effects
- Appreciating the human voice
- Planning a podcast

Choosing Sounds

You want to add sound with care, making sure it fits the story, fits the other media in the story, adds to the mix rather than detracts from it, and has spark, clarity, and meaning. Sound, more than any other media, can:

- **Set the tone of your story.** For example, a slow, somber rhythm can portray a gloomy topic, such as a funeral. A light, airy rhythm can portray frivolity.
- **Focus the listener's attention.** The sound of a loud pop, a siren, or a whistle will draw the reader more into the topic.
- **Add tension.** As the story builds, the added sounds can also build with dramatic tension. For example, a drum beat can start out slowly and then quicken in time to match the pace of the story.
- **Add comic relief.** Just think of all the honks and cymbal crashes, neighing horses, and sliding whistle sounds that coincide with silly actions in slapstick comedy films.
- **Signify the beginning and end of the story.** Especially for podcasts, music cues the listener, focuses attention on the beginning, and then cues the listener again when the podcast is ending. For the last few seconds of the podcast, you can fade in the same music that started the podcast to subtly let the listener know the end is near.
- **Brand your content.** Using the same audio tracks, such as the beginning and ending music, helps brand your Web content, along with any logos or other imagery you have designed to make the work unique.

To help you assess what sounds you might choose and how they will contribute to your Web stories, you need to know a few characteristics of sound. Let's start with the properties of sound.

If music be the food of love, play on.

—Shakespeare, *Twelfth Night*

Dimensions of Sound

Sound is complex and affects listeners on multiple levels. On one level, sound is energy. The jingles on a tambourine (**FIGURE 5.1**) produce vibrations that travel through air to the listener's ears. On other levels, sound conveys rhythms, tells stories, evokes emotions, and recalls memories. Music is a language in itself. It communicates to your readers—sometimes with subtle whispers and sometimes with screeching shouts. Your voice has more power, significance, and flexibility than any other media.

FIGURE 5.1
Tambourine jingles
produce vibrations that
travel through air.

It's helpful to review a few terms you may already know to help assess whether sound works for a particular Web story. You also want to develop a good vocabulary so you can critique how sound affects Web content when you're working with others. Consider the following terms when you're working with sound:

- **Pitch.** The perception of whether a sound is high or low. Sound waves are measured in hertz (Hz); the faster the frequency, the more hertz and the higher the pitch. Treble refers to high frequency, whereas bass refers to low frequency.

- **Amplitude.** The loudness or softness of sound. Amplitude can be measured by the change in air pressure or the movement of molecules. Your personal perception of loud or soft is relative and cannot be measured.

- **Acoustics.** How sound travels through the environment.

- **Rhythm and beat.** Patterns made with sound by grouping notes with accented and unaccented beats. For example, a jazz tune will have a completely different rhythm and beat than a country music ballad.

- **Timbre.** The tone of the sound. Sounds, like words, have textures and qualities, such as somber, smooth, rough, hollow, and so forth. For example, if you compare the same note coming from a violin and a tuba, the violin can sound sad, whereas the tuba can sound happy.

Close your eyes and
listen to one of your
favorite songs. Write a few
sentences to describe it
in terms of the timbre of
the music, the rhythms,
the pitch, and your
perceptions of loudness
and softness.

Types of Audio for the Web

For Web stories, you can add sound in as you add text and images, or you can record it separately and add it in later. Here are the different types of sound you can consider adding to your Web content:

- **Recorded voice.** Voice narration, including interviews, dialogues, monologues, instructions, poetry, songs, and so forth.
- **Sound effects.** Typically short excerpts of sound used to represent action noises, such as doors creaking or sirens blaring. Many audio software programs include a variety of royalty-free sound effects. You can also make your own sound effects using Foley techniques (see the sidebar "Jack Foley and the Foley Techniques" later in this chapter).
- **Music.** Songs and tunes, typically played in the background, to enhance content.

Adding Sound Effects

Watch a tense fight scene from an action-adventure movie. Watch the scene with the sound on first. Then watch it again with the sound off. What differences do you notice? Many times, without the sound, you can tell that fists aren't really connecting with faces and stomachs!

The sound of a door slamming can hit your listener with much more impact than text or an audio narration that says a door slammed shut. On the other hand, if there's no literal or metaphorical reference in the story for the drama of a door slamming shut, this sound effect will just confuse your readers.

Finding just the right sound effect, or creating it, is an art. Sound designer Ben Burtt created Chewbacca's Wookiee funky roar in Star Wars with a mix of animal sounds (http://filmsound.org/starwars/). You can make the sound of sliding doors opening and shutting by sliding a sheet of paper in and out of an envelope. Body punches and cracks can be created by thumping a cabbage or snapping a piece of celery.

JACK FOLEY AND THE FOLEY TECHNIQUES

Venessa Theme Ament tells us in The Foley Grail: The Art of Performing Sound for Film, Games, and Animation (Focal Press, 2009) that Jack Foley was a man of many talents. He worked as a stuntman and double in the film business before becoming an assistant director. He was one of the first sound artists to add sound to silent movies. Initially, there was only one soundstage where musicians, singers, and sound people like Jack worked to add the sounds of hands clapping, feet moving, clothes rustling, and so forth. Among other objects, Foley used various kitchen gadgets, a cane, and a cloth he kept in his back pocket for sound effects. Today, Foley artists use a separate recording room.

When deciding on sound effects, here are a few guidelines:

- **Less is more.** Use sound effects sparingly. If you pile them on, listeners might feel like there's a three-ring circus going on in the story.

- **Use effects that enhance the story.** Don't be tempted to use a sound effect just because you like it; make sure it fits in well with the content.

- **Time properly.** If the sound track doesn't match the visuals, listeners are pulled out of the story. You can watch almost any software tutorial and recognize that the developer used a canned sound effect for keys typing, and the sound of the keystrokes doesn't match the visual display of the characters that are typed. It's similar to bad lip-synching.

- **Set the right volume.** You don't want to startle listeners or hurt their eardrums with loud noise. If the sound is too soft, listeners will stop paying attention to the story while they're straining to hear if the sound effect is a fog horn or a cow lowing in an empty pasture. You don't want listeners to stop listening and fiddle with the volume control.

In addition, don't be afraid to make your own sound effects using only your voice. There's a little Bobby McFerrin in everyone! Let's explore the power of the human voice.

The Human Voice

The voice is as unique as fingerprints and more powerful and captivating than any musical instrument. A child can make a room full of adults come running with a small, soft yelp. You naturally modulate the pitch, cadence, timbre, and volume of your speech, and thus, those listening can instantly sense emotion, tone, intensity, and the significance along with the meaning of the words. Your pauses and inflections, your word choice, and what you don't say help listeners read between the lines and understand much more than what is spoken out loud.

The rest of this chapter describes telling stories on the Web with the human voice, starting with planning a podcast.

Planning a Podcast

For your readers, a podcast can provide a refreshing oasis, a respite from a dry desert of words and images. If the story is clear and draws in the reader, congratulations. You're not making the reader read.

The storyboard or script for a podcast depends largely on the topic and the speakers. If you've watched many good speakers, you know that some can talk for a full hour without any notes or just by using a few words scribbled on

Go to www.storycorps.org and listen to several stories that appeal to you. Observe how simply the recordings are presented, with a single still image and a sentence or two of introduction. What works and doesn't work for you? Write a few sentences explaining your preferences.

an index card. Others need slides, scripts, and perhaps a teleprompter. Cooking show hosts have all the ingredients laid out on the table before them to prompt them as they describe how to make a dish. Whether you need to write the script verbatim or not, it's best to have a plan, a direction, and some of the verbiage scripted.

But how do you come up with story ideas for podcasts?

VOX HUMANA

Since 2003, StoryCorps, with the mission "to provide Americans of all backgrounds and beliefs with the opportunity to record, share, and preserve the stories of our lives," has interviewed more than 35,000 individuals from all walks of life (www.storycorps.org).

More recently, StoryCorps has begun animating a few of the audio stories. In 2005, StoryCorps interviewed the oral historian Studs Terkel. In the interview, Terkel talks about *vox humana*, which means the human voice. You can listen to the audio story at www.storycorps.org/listen/stories/studs-terkel. This story has also been animated. For a comparison, view the same audio story but with animation at www.storycorps.org/animation/the-human-voice. Which story did you like better? Did the animation add to or detract from the experience?

Capturing Audio Story Ideas

Close your eyes this very moment and relax. Try to think of an incident that happened some time in your past. What came to mind? Is there a story? Often, your very first thought is your best thought. Consider using this idea for an audio story.

You listen to and tell stories all the time. When someone asks, "What's up?" you have a story to tell. Your ancestors have passed down stories. You've collected stories from colleagues, friends, and enemies. Start by making lists of some of your favorites. Soon you'll have more story ideas than you have time to produce. Keep both pen and paper and your digital tools handy to write down all your ideas as they emerge.

Some of the best stories originate from memories, from stories you've already told a time or two: an embarrassing moment; an important lesson learned; a goal achieved; a funny, scary, or trying escapade; a rite of passage that didn't go well.

Review Chapter 4 for more ideas about how to brainstorm and capture ideas by yourself and with a collaborator.

Creating a Podcast Storyboard

You might ask why you would need a storyboard, which typically involves images, for an audio recording. Although the medium is audio, you still need to plan the parts of the story. What is the main theme? Write down the big picture—what the story is about. Plan the credits, the teaser, the introduction, the body or main story, the closing, and any music, images, sound effects, or talent you will incorporate.

Here are a few guidelines for creating your podcast:

- **Introduce the topic.** Include the introduction in the accompanying text for the podcast *and* in the audio narration. The introduction should succinctly tell what the audio is about and who it's for.

- **Write a teaser.** You can add the teaser to the accompanying text, leaving it out of the podcast, if that works best. The teaser differs from the introduction in that it portrays only a juicy taste of the story and makes the listener hungry for more.

- **Use images sparingly if at all.** Use images only if they add to the story. Remember that the voice alone conveys tone, mood, and meaning. You don't want anything to spoil the clarity of the story.

- **Pace the story.** Your listeners need a little time to absorb the spoken word. But also keep in mind that because audio moves in a linear fashion, your listeners can't dart around and speed forward. Don't try their patience with a pace that's too slow or a story that rambles.

> *Back then people closed their eyes and listened to music. Today, there's a lot of images that go with the music. A lot of music is crap, and it's all commercial and the images are all trying to sell the record.*
>
> —Neil Young

- **Add a partner.** Telling a story, or interviewing a speaker, adds interest and depth to a story. Listen to radio ads. When there are two speakers, the information doesn't seem as dull and the sales pitch doesn't feel as monotonous. If only one person is telling the story, having a listener in the background chuckling or just saying, "Yes, I remember that," will add warmth to the story.

- **Keep the story short.** You can tell a gripping story in just two or three minutes. If you have any doubts about this, listen to stories produced by StoryCorps. If the topic is dry, a five-minute podcast is too long. If you have a lot of information to cover for a topic, consider producing several separate, short podcasts rather than one long one.

FIGURE 5.2

Sample storyboard format
for a podcast.

Podcast Storyboard

Podcast Title	
Producer (Your Name)	
Artists (Photos)	
Composers (Music)	
Speakers	

Introduction—*Your Name, Podcast Title, Date*	**Images**	**Music/Jingles**
Teaser—*What this episode is about*		
Main Story—*Questions or main idea for your interview or story. Use back of form to provide more details.*		

The sample storyboard in **FIGURE 5.2** can help you plan your podcast. You can find a template for this storyboard, as well as a completed example, at www.write4web.com.

With your podcast storyboard in process, you'll need a few tips and techniques for scripting the dialogue or monologue.

Scripting Dialogue

Writing good dialogue is an art. Every spoken word has several jobs. It has to fit the context, show who is speaking, interest the listener, and move the story forward. Scripting the dialogue helps you to focus on creating clear and meaningful communication. You might find that you abandon the script once the recording is in full swing. But having written the script and practiced it, you'll make the recording much smoother. Without the script, you can spend a lot of time re-recording and editing.

If you are working with others, it's often best for speakers to write their own script. That way, when recording, all the dialogue sounds more natural.

Of course, there are a few common mistakes that can occur in every script. But you can avoid these errors by adhering to the suggestions described in the following sections.

STILTED LANGUAGE

Avoid clumsy, stuffy chatter that is too formal. If you've ever studied a foreign language, there's a good chance that during the initial classes you had to memorize a few stilted dialogues that didn't sound very natural. *Hello Isabel, how are you? I am fine, thank you, and how are you?*

The following example illustrates a stilted dialogue versus a more natural style.

STILTED DIALOGUE	POSSIBLE SOLUTION
Hello Cici. I have some news. Our little sister has just announced that she is getting married to Fred. This is hard to believe, because just last month Cici told us she would marry Jacob.	Hi Cici. Unreal! Last month Jake and this month Fred. Cici's got a revolving door for her fiancés!

INFORMATION DUMPING

Also known as *Dick Tracy Talk*, information dumping occurs when the speaker just dumps information on the listener that the speaker would not actually say. For example, lots of information dumping occurs in soap operas and crime scene TV shows. The writers get lazy, or the show has to fit into a 50-minute segment. As a result, details that should be shown otherwise are simply stuffed into conversations.

The following example illustrates information dumping.

INFORMATION DUMPING	THE PROBLEM
BEATRICE: First our youngest sister tells us she is marrying Fred, whom she just met a few weeks ago. Then she shows us her wedding dress, which she bought months ago when she thought she would marry Jeffrey. She's wearing Vera Wang. And here we are trying on bridesmaid dresses suitable for a square dance! CICI: Beatrice, our dresses aren't that bad. You are having a problem because you are the middle child and you feel mom and dad did not give you enough attention.	CICI and BEATRICE are sisters, so they are already aware of their birth order. They might complain about the dresses or gossip about their younger sister, but they would have already shared most of the information dumped in this dialogue.

SPEECHES

If you find that your script contains long paragraphs of dialogue for the speaker, you most likely have written a speech that will bore your listeners. Unless you're recording a soliloquy equivalent to Hamlet's *To Be or Not to Be,* it's best to break up speeches into a succession of short exchanges.

CHIT-CHAT

It's important with interviews to follow a few polite formalities. You might just ask, "How are you?" or talk about a recent accomplishment by the speaker or an event the speaker was involved in. But thereafter, you can delete any verbiage that is simply chatter and doesn't move the story forward.

Music conveys moods and images. Even in opera, where plots deal with the structure of destiny, it's music, not words, that provides power.

—Marcel Marceau

SPEAKERS ALL SOUND THE SAME

When all the speakers in a podcast use the same diction and syntax, not only does the dialogue become boring but it is unnatural. A 12-year-old Valley Girl doesn't sound anything like an adult from Texas. You wouldn't show all the elderly women in your stories sitting in rocking chairs, so don't make them all sound like Aunt Bee from *The Andy Griffith Show.*

Recording Guidelines

With a little practice and the right tools, you'll find the recording process easy. You'll want to set up ahead of time, and record a sample test. That way your speakers can simply relax and hopefully forget all about the mic.

Here are a few guidelines for capturing audio:

- **Choose a quiet place.** Just as the camera can capture unintended images, such as crumbs on a kitchen counter, the mic can capture noise you did not intend to capture. Choose a place to record that doesn't have any background noises, such as a fan whirring or a refrigerator humming. Turn off your cell phones and listen to the equipment you are using for any noise. Does the fan on your computer generate noise?

- **Use pauses.** Don't be afraid to use an instant of silence, like white space. Pauses are perfectly fine, as long as the listener doesn't feel you've fallen asleep or run into technical difficulties.

- **Keep papers quiet.** If you are following a script, make sure papers don't rustle.

- **Record in segments.** Recording several short segments can help ease the pain of repeating flubbed lines over and over again.

- **Avoid background lyrics.** If you've added background music and voice narration, make sure the background music doesn't contain lyrics that will overshadow the voice narration. In most cases, it's best to use instrumental music in the background.

- **Introduce the topic and talent.** Summarize the topic and introduce yourself, other speakers, artists, musicians, and so forth.

Empty vessels make the loudest sound.

—Plato

- **Use a good microphone.** Don't use the built-in mic on your computer; it will sound muffled and echoed. If your mic picks up hissing or popping noises when you say words that start with b, p, or s, try an inexpensive or homemade pop filter (for instructions see www.write4web.com).

- **Play back on several different devices.** Test the audio on several different playback machines before publishing it.

Interviewing Techniques

Watch any interview on TV and you'll have a good sense of the host's or reporter's style and methods. You'll want to tailor your own style for the topic, the speakers you will interview, and your audience's expectations. For a successful interview, start by writing down the goals for the interview, such as:

- Ask good questions.
- Get good stories told in an interesting manner.
- Use follow-up questions to further examine the interviewee's beliefs, hopes, fears, and so forth.
- Stay out of your speaker's way; let the speaker talk while you remain in the background.
- Direct the interview so it stays on the main topic.

Prepare for the Interview

Before the interview, determine what stories you are looking for and how you will direct the interview while it's progressing. Prepare for the interview so you can hit the ground running when the recording begins. Here are a few possible preparations:

- **Choose the topic.** What is the main theme? What topics and subtopics do you want to cover?
- **Decide the scope.** How long will the interview last? What perspective will your questions focus on?

- **Write down good questions.** As the interview progresses, you don't have to stick with the original line of questioning, but it's good to have expectations rather than winging it.
- **Determine the location of the interview.** Make sure you have a quiet, comfortable, well-lit room for the recording session; chairs that are comfortable; a table with glasses and a pitcher of water; and no distractions.

Stage Your Questions

Just like any conversation, the interview will likely start out a little cold and then heat up. You want the interview to heat up as quickly as possible, so you can get to the good parts. But if you begin with a question that's too personal or too intense, your speaker can freeze up at the beginning, making your entire interview cold.

Prepare your questions in two or three phases. For example:

- **First set of questions.** After introductions, ask neutral questions about events and timelines. Encourage the speaker to expand and explain feelings and ideas.
- **Second set of questions.** Encourage the speaker to dig deeper into the stories to explain why things happened and how they relate to other events.
- **Third set of questions.** Ask big-picture questions. What was the significance? How did this change you?

BEGIN WITH A MEMORY QUESTION

Memory questions tend to relax a speaker. Asking a speaker to remember an incident in the past is a good way to get speakers to forget that they are in an interview and to fall into storytelling. Ask the speaker to remember a time, especially a first time, to remember a place, to remember who, what, when, where, and why.

ASK FOR EXPLANATIONS

Draw out your speaker's story by prompting for more details. For example:

- What caused this event?
- Why did it happen?
- What occurred next?
- Can you describe the scene?
- How did you feel?

ASK FOR AN ASSESSMENT OR JUDGMENT

Asking speakers to review and evaluate an event helps them to generate more information:

- What was the happiest (funniest or saddest) memory?
- What was your biggest accomplishment?
- What actions would you change if you had a chance to relive those years?
- What mistakes did people make?
- What should people today remember about the event?

Refocus on the Big Picture

Let the speaker talk about the big picture, telling about what was good or bad, important or insignificant. Ask big-picture questions last to give the speaker a chance to sum up and make conclusions.

Interviewing Guidelines

When you interview, remember that your role is to direct the production, keep the speakers talking on topic, make sure everyone is comfortable, and avoid distractions. Here are a few suggestions:

Rock Hudson is a solid stepper; Tony Curtis has a brisk foot; Audie Murphy is springy; James Cagney is clipped.

—Jack Foley

- Introduce yourself and the speakers.
- Make sure everyone can be heard clearly and will be recorded clearly.
- Don't ask "yes" and "no" questions. Your interview will be much more interesting if you ask open questions like "What were you thinking about when..." or "Please describe what it was like to..."
- If it's a long interview, make sure everyone is comfortable. Ask the speakers if they want water, want to take a break, or want to stand up and stretch.
- You want speakers to be able to relax and tell their best stories. Watch your body language.
- Keep a steady pace with continuous questions. If you feel your subject is rambling off topic, politely say, "Could I ask another question?"
- Use your best manners and say "Thank you" when the interview is finished.
- Most important, remember to have fun! Your audience will enjoy the outcome if you and your speakers enjoy the process.

Challenges

The best way to get better at writing Web content is to write, write some more, and rewrite. The challenges in this chapter focus on working with sound.

Freewriting

The freewriting challenges in this chapter ask you to practice writing with sound in mind.

Freewriting works best when it is timed. If you tend to write quickly, set the timer for ten minutes. If you tend to take a little more time, give yourself 15 minutes. Remember that with freewriting you don't need to worry about accuracy, grammar, spelling, and so forth.

VOICEMAIL MESSAGE

Write the script for a voicemail message. Make it serious or make it funny, but first decide:

1. Who is the audience?
2. What number has the caller dialed? Your home? Your cell? Your school?
3. When does the message play? Is it a message to leave a message? Is the caller on hold?

If you need a few ideas, Google *funny phone messages* and listen to a few on the Web.

INTERVIEW FOR A STORY

Interview a classmate or colleague, and then write his or her bio. First, write down a few questions you might ask to start. For example:

- How did you choose your current path of study?
- Who influenced you the most?
- What is your favorite artistic venue?
- When did you first discover your talents?

Second, write a follow-up set of questions that encourages your subject to expand on previous responses.

When the interview is over, take time to collect your thoughts. Begin writing.

Suggested Exercises

Exercises are longer projects that will take more time to complete. You can find more complete instructions, learning outcomes, and criteria for critiquing your work at www.write4web.com.

PLAN AN AUDIO STORY

Think of the idea for a three-minute story. Decide if you will tell a personal story yourself or interview another speaker. Will you use additional sound effects or music? Develop a storyboard for the podcast.

RECORD AN AUDIO STORY

Using your storyboard, produce the podcast.

Up Next

Now that you've reviewed guidelines for adding sound effects, music, and audio narration to your Web content, you can continue on with Chapter 6, "Writing Nonlinear, Interactive Stories." Chapter 6 discusses how to think interactively, manage content, and provide meaningful links to your Web stories.

6

Writing Nonlinear, Interactive Stories

The interactions built into your Web content can offer your readers a fantastic, custom journey on the Web. Interactive links can provide a pleasurable trip to meaningful information with satisfying speed and agility. On the flip side, some interactivity can leave readers feeling bored, frustrated, distrustful, overwhelmed, and exhausted. To provide the pleasurable ride, you'll need to work as an author *and* a designer as you develop content. You'll need to understand your readers, how they hunt for information, and what their needs and expectations are. Your readers won't be aware of how hard you've worked to get links just right, chunk information, and arrange intuitive navigational paths. That's good! Readers should click through the interactions without a thought about where the journey began, where they've been, or how they arrived at the final destination.

This chapter discusses how you can make sure readers have seamless, positive interactions with your Web content and covers:

- Managing content
- Adding positive interactions
- Telling nonlinear stories

Managing Content

The underlying structure of your Web content is the foundation you build on when you add interactivity. Whether you publish your work on an expansive Web site with multiple authors or you're working on a site where you are the sole author, content management will keep you sane and help you to give your readers a smooth path as they navigate the content. Here's where you need to wear the hat of an information architect while you lay the groundwork as you organize and manage content.

You'll first need to find a system or organization that works for you, for your readers, and for the content. Determine whether your audience is composed of both experts and novices. Do you need to include beginner levels, intermediate levels, and advanced levels of information? How much information should appear, at a glance, for your readers? How will you chunk information, dividing the content so it's just right for the reader?

Here are four steps you can take while building a strong foundation:

1. **Plan.** Research how others have organized similar content. Visit the library and observe how the Dewey Decimal System categorizes content. Look at similar Web sites. Go to grocery stores and drugstores and notice how items are stored on shelves. (But beware! Grocery stores aren't always looking after their customers. A lot of junk food is placed conveniently at eye level.)

2. **List and categorize.** Start making lists of topics you regularly write about, and then sort them into categories. After your first round of organizing, broaden the categories to make room for later additions. For example, if you had a list of the topics blueberries, strawberries, and huckleberries, you initially might categorize the topics under berries. But then where would you put pineapples and mangos if you write about them later?

NARROW CATEGORY	BROAD CATEGORY
Berries	Fruit
blueberries	blueberries
strawberries	strawberries
huckleberries	huckleberries
	pineapple

3. **Decide what choices readers want.** What choices will you offer your readers? How many choices will you provide? Is there a sequence for the choices? If so, which will be presented first? What does the reader see to know that there's a choice? When you have a better idea of how you want information to appear to your readers, you'll know how to group topics and divide large segments of information into smaller chunks.

try this

Select 15 to 20 photos from your private collection that you will show to a family member, such as your mother, a sibling, or a close cousin. Sort the photos into several categories and write down the names of the categories. Decide how you might show them if you put them online. What is the organizational structure? Did you organize by time, by event, or by who was in the photo?

4. **Choose a shallow hierarchy.** It's better to organize topics with a hierarchy that's wide and shallow rather than narrow and deep. This will help you to keep all links visible and prevent readers from feeling like they are spelunking in subterranean caves.

Once you have a plan and a system for managing content, you can plan how you will add interactivity. Interactivity usually consists of *hot links*, or text and images that are wired with hyperlinks to send your reader to another view of information. Of course your reader will also navigate your content with elements that are intrinsic to the design of the Web site, such as menus, links on the sidebar, the search engine, and the site map. You may or may not have control over the site's design. However, you do have control over how your links look and what they link to, which you'll learn about next.

Follow your bliss and the universe will open doors where there were only walls.

—Joseph Campbell

Adding Links

By adding links to your text and images, you open up whole new worlds for your reader. Not only can you link to content that you've authored, but you can link to anything on the Web. It's easy to go a little crazy and start sending the reader off in a hundred different directions, just because you can. But show a little restraint and keep your readers focused.

The link is like a door waiting to be opened. The link needs to fit the context and structure where it resides and provide a small window to what's on the other side of the door.

Ideally, your readers see a link that looks promising, choose the link, and wooosh! they are whisked off to another page of content that meets their expectations. Preferably, if you're linking to another page, the link text matches the title of the page (**FIGURE 6.1**).

FIGURE 6.1
The link text should be a window to the link destination.

Lagomorphs
Posted on July 17, 2011 by Chelsea

Rabbits, hares and pikas are mammals and classified as Lagomorphs.

Lagomorphs differ from rodents in that:

- they have four incisors in the upper jaw, rather than two
- they are herbivorous, whereas many rodents eat meat

Pikas
Posted on July 17, 2011 by Chelsea

Pikas are small mammals from the Lagomorpha family. They have short limbs, rounded ears, and short tail. Pikas are typically six to nine inches long, they are crepuscular, and like to live on rocky mountain sides, where there are numerous crevices. The young are born after 25 to 30 days of gestation.

Link Wisely

By offering choices to your readers, you give them more control over what they view. As a result, you give up some of your control over how the content appears to readers. Before adding a link, you should determine if your readers truly want the choice. Sometimes autocratic rule is best, and you should dictate the path that readers take. For example, if there's a logical progression, such as a recipe, there's no point in asking the reader to open another view for ingredients or steps. You'll simply show the information without links, step by step.

Links help the reader to see the big picture and to follow the main flow of thought without distraction. Wiki pages, for example, offer general information about a topic and then provide a list of links that serve as portals to further information. Link information that supports, complements, or enhances the main topic, such as:

- **Examples.** Samples, case studies, and scenarios that supplement the topic.
- **Tutorials.** Lessons that provide extra remedial help for beginners or advanced lessons for experts.
- **Sidebars.** Content that would be considered marginalia in a magazine, such as interesting facts, short human-interest stories, or commentary from luminaries in the field of the topic.
- **Related topics.** Information about comparable subjects.
- **Resources.** Supporting white papers, reports, critiques, analyses, bibliographies, and other background information.

Adding insignificant links should be avoided, so it's best not to do anything like:

- Add links spontaneously because you can.
- Add links because you run out of room or don't want your readers to get tired of scrolling.

Links don't require a lot of effort to incorporate, and it's easy to begin spontaneously adding more and more links while feeling good about how you're giving your readers extra valuable choices. But be wary of your good intentions, which can backfire and send your readers on a wild ride (**FIGURE 6.2**). It's crucial to plan your approach and add links systematically.

> **Prepare to Evacuate**
>
> Posted on July 17, 2011 by Chelsea
>
> Step Five – Make a list of what you'll take
>
> Write down what you'll pack in the car and how you'll pack it. You won't want to just stick the crystal goblets on the dashboard! And the fish need to be far enough away from the cat. Consider each important item and how it fits into your big suitcase or your car. One good lesson we learned while evacuating was to store things in good containers. We had many items neatly placed in clear blue plastic Rubbermaid bins. As we dashed about the house in the fifteen minutes we had to get out, we dumped the original contents from the bins and then filled them with photo albums, which we then transported to the car.

FIGURE 6.2
Be wary of sending your readers on a wild ride with too many links.

Write Meaningful Text for Links

The link text or image needs to let readers know where they'll land after clicking the link. Common mistakes authors make include using link names such as *click here* or *for more information* or *see also*. These links are unacceptable on many levels. They don't tell readers what the link points to. They add meaningless, repetitive text and begin to sound like a broken record, without providing readers any differentiation when making choices. In addition, links like *click here* do not follow accessibility guidelines and are inconsiderate for readers with vision impairments (see the sidebar "Click here. Click here. Click here.").

CLICK HERE. CLICK HERE. CLICK HERE.

In "Guidelines for Accessible and Usable Web Sites: Observing Users Who Work with Screen Readers," authors Mary Theofanos and Janice Redish describe how visually impaired users work with screen readers (www. redish.net/content/papers/interactions.html). The reader software lists all the links on the screen in a separate window. Therefore, if the author has added multiple links named *click here* and *more*, the list is filled with the terms *click here, click here, click here* and *more, more, more.*

The following example provides a link that is not meaningful, as well as a possible solution.

NOT MEANINGFUL	SOLUTION
For more information about the Millennium Falcon click here.	Han Solo and Chewbacca commanded the Millennium Falcon.

The following example shows a link that doesn't clearly show readers what they'll get when they choose it. You don't want readers to feel like they're on a mystery tour. This is especially true for interactions that take more time, such as downloading software, audio files, or PDFs. Readers become completely frustrated when they don't get what they expect.

CONFUSING LINK	SOLUTION
Download more information about our company.	A print version of our company brochure is available.

Keep Link Text Brief

Link the smallest amount of text that makes sense. Don't link long phrases or whole sentences. If you want the reader to take an action, link the action verbs. If you only need to provide a list of possible topics for further reading, just provide a linked list.

TOO MUCH	SOLUTION
Supplies can be ordered for this class at the university store.	Order supplies at the university store.

Don't Explain Links

Don't go out of your way to explain the link or the location where the reader lands after clicking on the link. Your readers just want to get their needs met and couldn't care less about all the details you had to take into account to get them there.

The following sample shows a link with too much text, which tells the reader information about the link destination. The solution is to remove this information.

TOO MUCH	SOLUTION
Visit our homepage at www.campysongs.net for a list of songs you can sing by the campsite fire.	For fun campfire songs, visit campysongs.net.

ISAAC ASIMOV ON PORTABLE DEVICES AND INTERACTIVITY

Speaking to the 1989 American Booksellers Association, Isaac Asimov asked the audience to imagine a device that could:

- Go anywhere
- Was totally portable
- Didn't need electric energy

In addition, Asimov said that this device would never be surpassed because "it represents the minimum technology with the maximum interaction you can have" (www.ku.edu/~sfcenter/library.htm). Have you guessed what he was talking about? A book!

Don't Add Shovelware

Instructional designers use the derisive term *shovelware* for Web content designed for another medium, such as printed books, and stuffed on the Web without changing the design, interactivity, and so forth to follow Web conventions. It's as though the author shoveled content from one medium to another. Shovelware is easy to spot. It lacks appropriate links. Sometimes the only links are those that turn pages. Sometimes you find a pile of PDF files shoveled into the content.

On the Web, *page-turner* is also a derisive term. If you're an author of a printed book, you would be thrilled to hear that your novel is a page-turner. However, on the Web it refers to content that was not well thought out. The organization is linear, so readers must tediously scroll and scroll and scroll, or click the *next* link again and again. Turning pages, in this case, can make readers feel like trained seals, getting a fish every time they flap their flippers to change the page.

Test the Links

Ask someone who fits your persona to test the links. (See "Develop a Persona" in Chapter 1 for more information about personas.) Web content changes from moment to moment, so periodically you should check links to make sure they still work. Provide the tester with a list of things to check, such as:

- **Links that misfire.** Links that result in an error message or land you in the wrong spot, or round-trip links that don't return you to the same spot at which you started.
- **Broken links.** Links that don't work at all.
- **Confusing links.** Links with text that doesn't clearly tell what the link points to.
- **Gratuitous links.** Links that point to information that the reader already knows or doesn't have any interest in. For example, the link provides a definition for a word understood by your reader.

Nonlinear, Interactive Stories

Linear stories move from beginning to middle to end, or from point A to point B to point C. Think of novels, movies, radio, and TV shows where viewers have little or no interactivity. The narrative of the story might jump around in time. For example, the story might begin in the middle of an event's time frame and then flash back in time to what caused the event. But the reader follows the author's chosen path, without interaction.

With nonlinear, interactive stories, readers become active participants, making choices that determine the progression of the story. Web content, games, and even books such as dictionaries and encyclopedias are all nonlinear and interactive. If you want to look up zemstvo in the dictionary, you don't have to scramble through all of the pages for A through Y to get to it. Books were a great improvement upon prior forms of publishing, such as the cuneiform tablets (**FIGURE 6.3**) and scrolls. The difficulty in searching for information in the middle of a scroll is akin to the difficulty in finding a song in the middle of a cassette tape.

FIGURE 6.3
Cuneiform script on a clay tablet.

Telling stories with a nonlinear structure and interactivity is not a new idea. Argentine writer Julio Cortázar published *Hopscotch* (Pantheon, 1987) in English in 1966. Instructions in the beginning of the book tell readers they can read the novel from front to back, in a linear progression, or they can skip around the chapters using another recommended progression.

You can find many interactive stories on the Web. A great example is "To Be A Drum" at www.storylineonline.net. Along with the audio story, which is beautifully narrated by James Earl Jones, you'll find information about the author, Evelyn Coleman, and the illustrator, Aminah Brenda Lynn Robinson, and plenty of related activities.

Digital storytelling with interactivity is an emerging field. Whether it's fiction or nonfiction, journalists, educators, businessmen and women, and people from all walks of life are mastering tools and art forms to tell spellbinding and poignant stories in novel ways.

What interactive stories will you add to the mix?

With the poem "Thirteen Ways of Looking at a Blackbird," Wallace Stevens offers 13 stanzas, each with separate visions and blackbirds. Read the poem at www.poetryfoundation.org/poem/174503. Then write a short poem or several short paragraphs that describe 13 ways of looking at someone or something.

Challenges

The best way to get better at writing Web content is to write, write some more, and rewrite. The challenges in this chapter focus on interactivity.

Freewriting

The freewriting challenge in this chapter asks you to practice writing by adding links and choices with your readers in mind.

Freewriting works best when it is timed. If you tend to write quickly, set the timer for ten minutes. If you tend to take a little more time, give yourself 15 minutes. Remember that with freewriting you don't need to worry about accuracy, grammar, spelling, and so forth.

GAME SCENE

Write a game scene for 12 year olds. Incorporate the following suggestions, or come up with your own setting, players, and goals.

- **Setting.** A haunted Victorian house in the city where you live.
- **Characters.** Player, villain, athlete, owner of the house, fitness instructor.
- **Goal.** To stay out of harm's way and outsmart the villain by solving puzzles, staving off menaces, and figuring out how the other characters can help.

WILD RIDE

Describe a time when you felt you were on a *wild ride*, on the Internet or anywhere at all.

Suggested Exercise

Exercises are longer projects that will take more time to complete. You can find more complete instructions, learning outcomes, and criteria for critiquing your work at www.write4web.com.

FRACTURED FAIRY TALE

Choose a traditional fairy tale that you want to fracture or tell with some sort of strange twist. The goal of this exercise is to write the tale in segments with links, offering the reader choices for how the story progresses. Here are some suggestions:

- *Goldilocks and the Three Bears*
- *Little Red Riding Hood*
- *The Three Little Pigs*

Start by deciding on the moral of the tale. You might have three morals, depending on which path the reader chooses. Traditional tales have morals such as:

- Don't trust someone who flatters you.
- Don't be conceited.
- The race is not to the swift, nor the battle to the strong (the tortoise can win).

The moral that you choose can be fractured too. Dorothy Parker is famous for saying, "No good deed goes unpunished."

Write the fairy tale with three different endings that are linked to either three different points of view or three different morals. For example, one path of the story might tell *Goldilocks and the Three Bears* from Mama Bear's point of view, another from Goldilocks's, and the third from Baby Bear's.

Up Next

There's a lot to consider when adding interactivity to your Web content. If you're ready to continue, let's move on to Chapter 7, "Writing Succinctly," which concentrates on steps you can take to delete needless words and strip out clutter.

Chapter

7

Writing Succinctly

Succinct writing takes practice, skill, and discipline. With practice, you get better and better at demanding that every syllable, word, phrase, sound, and image moves your story forward. With skill, you learn to identify blather, happy talk, redundancies, and tangents that don't belong in the story. With discipline, you find the courage and strength to ruthlessly annihilate all but the most vital parts of your work. Some of the best writing of your career will die on the cutting room floor.

This chapter provides pointers on writing succinctly, including how to:

- Stay focused
- Distill content
- Eliminate excess

- Kill happy talk
- Stop hype

Stay Focused

With your red pen in hand, you're ready to start crossing out words. But wait; before you start slashing your words, look at the story as a whole and examine its structure. You'll most likely find that there are entire sections to cut—content that wanders off and contains tangential information that doesn't support the main idea or storyline.

Before you look for clutter at the sentence or word level, first scrutinize the design and structure of your story.

If any man wishes to write in a clear style, let him be first clear in his thoughts; and if any would write in a noble style, let him first possess a noble soul.

—Goethe

Work with Architecture

As an author, you become the architect and master builder of your Web content. You'll first draw the blueprint, and then you'll build the story to fit the plan. Your blueprint can be an outline, a list, a storyboard, or whatever works best for you. Make sure the architecture suits the style and genre of the story: For example, an architect's design for a classic Craftsman bungalow might have built-in cabinets and furniture, but it won't have Greek columns or a portico. Your design for instructions might have steps for a process, but it might not feature a comparison of products.

Chapter 10, "A Refresher on Rhetorical Modes," suggests how you might plan and organize several types of Web content. If you tenaciously stick to your plan, you'll already have the structure for your story cleanly built.

Distill Your Content

If your story feels too loose and boxy, read it again to see if it needs to be condensed and tightened. Put on your architect's hat and look over the plan. Maybe you designed a house with ten rooms, but you really only need seven.

So many Web articles start out with *10 Ways to* (get rich, catch a liar, sleep better, and so forth) or *10 Reasons for*. If you are writing such an article, don't arbitrarily choose a number before you understand the reasons or ways you will include. Do you truly need *ten* ways? Review the content to see if some points can be combined or distilled.

For any Web content that you are struggling with, write down the main idea in three sentences. If you can't, sit back and think about what you meant to write about. Then try again.

Be Positive

Your tone will be lighter and you'll use fewer words if you write positive rather than negative statements.

The following example illustrates how your word count decreases with positive statements.

NEGATIVE	POSITIVE
Do not write negative statements. (5 words)	Write positive statements. (3 words)

Trust the Reader

Remember that your readers are intelligent, sentient, capable beings. No one likes to be told what they already know. Readers will resent hand-holding and excessive instructions. They especially don't want interface elements named and described, such as radio buttons, drop-down menus, and expanding and collapsing contents.

TOO MUCH	BETTER
Access the Amazon Web site at www.amazon.com. Locate the Shop All Departments menu on the left side of the screen. Click the Kindle drop-down menu, and then choose eBooks. (29 words)	Access Amazon.com and choose Kindle > eBooks. (6 words)

Choose Anglo-Saxon Words

The English language has so many choices! Have you ever wondered why English has so many more words than French or German? For instance, have you ever questioned why sheep, cow, swine, deer, and chicken are called mutton, beef, pork, venison, and pullet at dinner? You can find the answers to these questions, as well as a brief history of the evolution of the English language, in Richard Lederer's *The Miracle of Language* (Pocket Books, 1991). Lederer explains how our language began in 400 AD when the Angles, Saxons, and Jutes settled in England. The biggest shift in English came when William the

Prose is architecture, not interior decoration, and the Baroque is over.

—Ernest Hemingway

Conqueror sailed over from Normandy and became king at the Battle of Hastings in 1066. The Normans gained power, but they were outnumbered. They wisely didn't demand that everyone speak their language, so French words were blended with English words. Another shift occurred during the Renaissance, when a surge of Latin and Greek terms entered the English language.

Some say English is a mutt, a blend of words from many languages and cultures. And it's still evolving!

TABLE 7.1 shows examples of word choices for a few common verbs and nouns. Notice that the Anglo-Saxon words are short and powerful—only one syllable. If you want to write with strength and brevity, choose Anglo-Saxon words over their French and Latin or Greek counterparts.

TABLE 7.1 CHOICES FOR COMMON WORDS

ANGLO-SAXON	FRENCH	LATIN/GREEK
ask	interrogate	question
dead	deceased	defunct
end	finish	conclude
thin	spare	emaciated

ONE-SYLLABLE WORDS

Stephen King points out in his memoir, *On Writing* (Scribner, 2000), that several great authors use simpler, smaller words. He illustrates this with a sentence written by Steinbeck in *The Grapes of Wrath*:

"Some of the men were kind because they hated what they had to do, and some of them were angry because they hated to be cruel, and some of them were cold because they had long ago found that one could not be an owner unless one were cold."

King points out that although the sentence is 50 words long, 39 of the words have only one syllable, and the other 11 have two syllables.

If you read Steinbeck's novels, you'll notice that he uses many Anglo-Saxon words.

Eliminate Excess Words

You truly can cut half the words from your original document by using other elements. Use titles and subtitles. Or, use certain formats, such as bullets, so you don't have to use whole sentences. When you use a bullet list, see if you are repeating words in each bullet item, such as "how to." Instead, start the overall list with how to rather than putting how to in every bullet item.

OMIT WORDS

Steve Krug, in *Don't Make Me Think* (New Riders, 2000), pays homage to rule number 17, *Omit needless words,* in *The Elements of Style* (Allyn & Bacon, 1979) by Strunk and White. Krug, however, places a big black X over the word *needless,* following the principle and omitting one word.

Strunk and White's collaboration on *The Elements of Style* is unusual. E.B. White was first introduced to the book as a student at Cornell in 1919. Strunk was his English professor, and the textbook was required reading. In 1957, years after Strunk's death, White was asked to revise *The Elements of Style.*

Remove Redundancies

It's fairly easy to let words creep in that just repeat what is already evident from a similar word. Watch for phrases in which words are often paired together. For example:

- past experience
- cease and desist
- close proximity
- basic fundamentals
- free gift

- begin to initiate
- a burning fire
- earlier, previous
- same exact thing

When words are scarce they are seldom spent in vain.

—William Shakespeare

Shorten Inflated Phrases

Be careful when using phrases that come to you quickly because you've heard them or read them many times. They often are stuffed with needless words.

The following examples show inflated phrases and how you can shorten them:

INFLATED PHRASES	BETTER
On account of the fact of	Because
In order to	To
As a matter of fact	Truly
It goes without saying	(Delete the whole phrase)
All of a sudden	Suddenly

Keep Verbs Alive

try this

Find a quiet place and read your work out loud. As you're reading, pay attention to phrases you stumble over, places you want to speed up, or anything that's hard to say. It's likely that you'll find words you can delete or refine.

When verbs are passive or vague, you add more words to get your meaning across. Watch for nondescriptive verbs, such as *do* or *get*. See "Keep Verbs Active" in Chapter 2 for more information.

The following example shows a sentence with lifeless verbs versus vital verbs.

LIFELESS VERBS	VITAL VERBS
The vase was bumped into by Jeffrey, and it got wobbly for a moment and then went crashing to the floor. (21 words)	Jeffrey bumped the vase, making it wobble and then crash to the floor. (13 words)

Ax Adverbs and Adjectives

Don't spend your energy building up nouns and verbs with adjectives and adverbs. Instead, choose strong nouns and strong verbs. Adjectives like *very* and *little* sap rather than strengthen the nouns they modify. Adverbs like *very*, *suddenly*, *extremely*, *phenomenally*, *quickly*, *immediately*, and so on slow down the sentence and dilute the emphasis.

WEAK	STRONG
Very, very tired	spent
Studied extremely hard	crammed
Smelled extremely bad	stank
Did a phenomenal job	excelled

Omit Wuss and Weasel Words

Wuss words not only add clutter, they make your Web content sound tentative. Weasel words make your Web content sound insincere, sneaky, or ambiguous. Your readers will feel a lack of confidence in the tone of the work and begin to question what you are saying. Make sure you don't begin your sentences tentatively or give halfhearted reasons for your arguments. Especially, don't use qualifiers such as *very* and *rather*. Make the nouns they modify stronger.

Look for these words to cut:

- seems
- possibly
- rather
- sort of
- may
- generally
- pretty
- kind of
- perhaps
- apparently
- relatively

Substitute "damn" every time you're inclined to write "very"; your editor will delete it and the writing will be just as it should be.

—Mark Twain

Omit Arrogant and Snooty Words

When an author begins with IMHO (in my humble opinion), the content that follows is typically highly opinionated and not at all humble. It's good to have an attitude and to state your opinions. However, when you have done so, reread the work to make sure your tone isn't arrogant or patronizing, or couched in extra words, such as *obviously*. *Obviously* obviously sounds disdainful.

Here are a few words to delete:

- relatively
- indeed
- certainly
- obviously
- of course
- surely
- needless to say
- exactly

Kill Happy Talk

In the 1990s, almost all home pages began: Welcome to *<the site or company name>*. Web designers are smarter now. They recognize that readers don't need a welcoming committee. Skip the formalities and jump straight to the important content. (See the sidebar "Must Happy Talk Die?")

Readers also don't want to be congratulated when they spend their hard-earned money on products and services. The introductory text of many product user guides starts out just so, congratulating viewers for their savvy purchase. Although this acclamation might have been OK a decade ago, now readers just find it arrogant, condescending, and annoying.

MUST HAPPY TALK DIE?

Jakob Nielsen calls the introductory text on Web pages blah-blah text, and he says, "Kill the welcome mat" ("Blah-Blah Text: Keep, Cut, or Kill?" www.useit.com/alertbox/intro-text.html). Steve Krug, in *Don't Make Me Think*, calls it happy talk and says, "Happy talk must die."

Generally, Web readers don't care for small talk. However, there are a few cases where sociable chit-chat works well, and you might be criticized if you completely strip it out. For example, if your content is in response to a hot line or technical issues, the reader might feel that your answers are cold or curt without adding a little happy talk. The same is true if you are a teaching assistant or teacher adding content to Moodle or some other online forum. Students can interpret brevity as aloofness, or they might feel as though you don't like them.

Stop Hype

Don't make your readers feel like you are a used car salesman or selling snake oil. Your readers' radar for sales pitches is sensitive, and they will shut down in a heartbeat if they sense the slightest inclination of a sales pitch. Even if you are selling products or services, describe and educate your readers with a straightforward style and tone rather than marketing fluff and hyperbole.

Here are a few phrases to avoid:

- At the touch of a button
- The best thing since sliced bread
- It's just perfect for ...
- Limited time offer

Here are a few examples of product phrases that promote benefits without exaggerated claims:

- Offers a 3.5-inch display
- Launches in 5 seconds or less
- Uses standard AA batteries

Challenges

The best way to get better at writing Web content is to write, write some more, and rewrite. The challenges in this chapter focus on writing concisely.

Freewriting

The following freewriting challenges ask you to practice writing short, distilled content. Freewriting works best when it is timed. If you tend to write quickly, set the timer for ten minutes. If you tend to take a little more time, give yourself 15 minutes. Remember that with freewriting you don't need to worry about accuracy, grammar, spelling, and so forth.

SIX-WORD NOVEL

Write a short, short story using six words. Hemingway wrote this one:
For sale: baby shoes, never used.

TWEET

Write three messages that you could post on Twitter. You're allowed up to 140 characters.

Suggested Exercise

Exercises are longer projects that will take more time to complete. You can find more complete instructions, learning outcomes, and criteria for critiquing your work at www.write4web.com.

REVISE WEB CONTENT

Choose any home page or Web content that contains "happy talk." Revise it, removing introductions, social niceties, and any other paragraphs, words, or syllables that are unnecessary and don't move the story forward.

Up Next

Now that you have some pointers on how to write succinctly, you can move on to the next chapter. Chapter 8, "Writing with Style and Good Grammar," explains the differences between having a style and writing with good grammar, and includes some advice on how to avoid the most common grammatical errors.

8

Writing with Style and Good Grammar

What first comes to mind when you hear the words *style* and *grammar*? For style, perhaps you think about stylish people, like Coco Chanel or Thelonious Monk. Chanel is noted for her classic simplicity and especially for introducing The Little Black Dress. Monk's improvisational style as a jazz pianist carried over to his attire. He could pull off wearing a classic suit with a Mandarin hat and sunglasses. For grammar, you're more likely to think of a schoolmarm, the stereotyped prim and proper English teacher, brandishing a ruler and wearing thick knee socks, ugly shoes, a pleated skirt, and a starched white blouse. However, did you know that the word glamour is derived from grammar? To learn more about how style and grammar are related to glamour, read on.

This chapter covers:

- The difference between style and grammar
- Choosing your style
- Why grammar rules
- Common mistakes to avoid

Style or Grammar?

What's the difference between style and grammar? Your style reflects your tastes and affinities. Your style reflects your sense of aesthetics. Your style reflects design choices for images and tables, such as colors, line weights, and font sizes. None of your stylistic choices can be considered wrong, although they can be considered inappropriate. Grammar is not as much a matter of choice as it is following a system that conforms to the structure of the English language. If you want your readers to believe in you, you'll follow the grammatical conventions expected by your readers. With grammar, there are conventions that you should know and mostly follow.

The following conventions illustrate style choices versus a grammar rule.

STYLE CHOICE	GRAMMAR RULE
Spell out numerals one through nine. Use integers for numerals 10 and greater. If a sentence begins with a number, spell it out.	Subjects and verbs must agree. A singular subject takes a singular verb. A plural subject takes a plural verb.

Choosing Your Style

Do you write e-mail or email? How do you represent time? For example, if it's seven o'clock in the morning, how do you write it? This is a matter of style, and you won't be faulted for bad grammar if you choose any of the following:

- Seven in the morning
- *7 ante meridiem*
- 7:00 AM
- 7 a.m.

However, many readers won't remember that AM is an acronym for *ante meridiem*, and you might lose them when they dash off to the dictionary.

What about telephone numbers? Do you use any of the following formats?

- (800) 123-4567
- 800/123-4567
- 800.123.4567

Keep the Audience in Mind

You might decide that using periods between the numerals in a phone number looks and feels modern and clean, so you adopt that style. However, you also need to consider whether or not the style best fits the audience and the medium. Periods are hard to see online, and if your audience mostly includes members of AARP, they will be more familiar with telephone numbers that use parentheses around the area code. The forward slash is also hard to see online.

The style you choose should fit your tastes and that of your audience.

Stay Consistent

Ralph Waldo Emerson said, "A foolish consistency is the hobgoblin of little minds." With Web writing, however, consistency is seldom foolish. Your readers will think you can't make up your mind if you spell out seven in the first half of your content and then switch to the numeral 7 for the second half. If you use an initial cap to write *Web*, don't suddenly start using a lowercase *web* version of the word.

If you're not following a style guide, create one to follow. Anytime you make a decision, no matter how small, notate the style choice and keep it in a document file. Soon you'll have a large collection of your style choices, which can be a handy reference.

Are you collaborating with a group of authors? If so, you definitely need to have standards, and make sure all authors either follow the standards or someone edits the work before publishing it.

Don't Get Too Creative

Choosing your style and following it can feel tedious, but the consistency allows your readers to skip through your sentences with a sense of comfort and trust. With style, you don't need to prove that you have a wild imagination. Your readers might get irritated if you decide to use uppercase and lowercase unconventionally or spell words like they belong on a license plate (for example, H8TE).

Using a Style Guide

Fortunately, you don't have to stop writing mid sentence every time you need to make a style choice. A professional style guide can help you determine the best way to represent almost any term or phrase in your Web content.

You have several style guides to choose from, and each sets a style for a particular audience. Each includes a massive reference of terms to show you how to capitalize, punctuate, underline, italicize, and so forth. Here are some of the more well-known style guides for American audiences:

- *The Chicago Manual of Style* **(University of Chicago Press, 2010).** This guide was first published in 1906. It is highly used and widely respected, and at 1026 pages (16th edition), it is one of the most comprehensive guides you'll find. It is written for a general audience.
- *The New York Times Manual of Style and Usage* **(Three Rivers Press, 2002).** This guide is used by writers and editors at the *New York Times*. At 384 pages, it's much less daunting than *The Chicago Manual of Style*.
- *The Associated Press Stylebook and Briefing on Media Law* **(Basic Books, 2011).** This guide is updated annually by Associated Press editors and used by newspapers, magazines, and broadcasters. The current edition has 448 pages.

- *MLA Handbook for Writers of Research Papers* **(MLA, 2009).** Referred to as the MLA Handbook, this guide is used in academia for scholarly papers.
- *The Elements of Style* **(Allyn & Bacon, 1979).** Written by William Strunk Jr. and E.B. White, this slim text is often thought of as a grammar book, but it's more about style. It's widely respected and only 105 pages. You can find a partial version of the guide online at www.bartleby.com/141.

If you work for a large corporation, you're likely to be handed a style guide to follow. For companies, it's especially important that all products and services are shown consistently in literature for employees and customers. Without a style guide, a product name—for example, WellBuilt7000—can be presented with a surprising number of variations.

If you are freelancing or have your own company, you'll impress your clients if you tell them that you work with a particular style guide or the style guide of their choice.

Your Personal Style

There are infinite choices to make when determining your personal style. This section suggests only a few style issues you might tackle and conventions you might adopt.

IS IT OK TO USE INTERNET LINGO?

Internet lingo, such as LOL (laughing out loud), and emoticons, such as :) (smiley face), have infiltrated the English language. It might be tempting to use the lingo in your Web content. The most important consideration is your audience and the type of message you are conveying. Certainly, when you are instant messaging or chatting, the lingo is appropriate, especially if you are in the workplace and stretched for time. You might get an instant message while you are on the phone and respond OTP (on the phone) to politely and quickly let your colleague know you can't chat at the moment.

But is Internet lingo appropriate for Web content, such as a blog post? As with all Web content, you need to gauge whether or not the lingo suits your audience.

If you decide Internet lingo is appropriate for your readers, make sure you use the most commonly accepted variations. (See the sidebar "LOL.")

LOL

A student shared in class that his mother thought that LOL meant *lots of love*. The family's beloved dog died, and the mother sent an email to close friends and family expressing the sad news about their pooch. Before she signed her name, she closed with LOL.

ARE CLICHÉS OK?

If a phrase sounds familiar and if you've heard it many times, it's a cliché.
A few examples include:

- Accidents will happen
- At the end of the day
- As if!
- Best kept secret
- Burning question
- Easier said than done
- Leave no stone unturned
- Lion's share
- Make ends meet
- Nipped in the bud
- Until the bitter end

Clichés are phrases that used to be novel and clever, such as the phrase *the bleeding edge of technology* that replaced *the leading edge of technology*. But very quickly, the novelty wears off, the phrase is overused, and the meaning becomes flat. Most critics advise writers to avoid clichés like the plague. They make your readers yawn and your work unimaginative and lazy.

For a different point of view, Randy Pausch wrote in *The Last Lecture* (Hyperion, 2008), "If at first you don't succeed ... try try a cliché." He loved clichés because what they so often express is right on the money. He also stated that teachers shouldn't be afraid of clichés, because today's students don't know them. It's a new world with a completely new audience.

ARE SWEAR WORDS OK?

If you're questioning whether or not it would be OK to use a particular swear word, it's probably best not to. Think of the adage *if you have to ask*. The key to whether off-color words work for your Web content, again, depends on the type of content and the audience.

For business content and the general public, swear words will never be appropriate, unless you want to get fired.

If you're writing a screenplay, the dialogue for certain characters, such as gangsters or hard-boiled detectives, might contain a swear word or two. It wouldn't be believable if these characters said *rats* or *darn it* when they faced adversity. (But you might have fun creating a seedy character who can't handle profanity.)

If you absolutely must use swear words to make your Web content convincing, consider using the convention used in comic books. Comic book authors use grawlixes for swear words. A grawlix is a dialogue bubble with a typographical representation of the swear word (@#$%&!).

ARE NEOLOGISMS OK?

Neologisms are words or phrases that have just been created. They are fun to use in speech, but do they work for your Web content? Will your audience appreciate them? This is a judgment call you'll have to make, depending on your readers and the context.

Here are a few examples of neologisms that are now well known and incorporated into the English language.

- Laser, the acronym for Light Amplification by Simulated Emission of Radiation.
- Podcast, which combines the words iPod and broadcast.
- Catch 22, the title and theme of Joseph Heller's novel.
- Google, uses the name of the search engine as a verb.

GENDER BIAS

Authors work hard to keep their language gender-neutral, but it isn't always easy. It's especially difficult when it comes to using pronouns. For so many years the personal pronoun *he* was accepted to represent both males and females. Then authors began to use *she* to represent both male and female to even the score somewhat. Some authors currently use both he and she, randomly, throughout their writings. Some readers find this method distracting.

A common approach to gender bias is to use the pronoun *they* and *their*. If this is your choice, it's a fine option, as long as you don't make a common grammatical error that often coincides with the use of *they* and *their*. Remember the grammatical rule that a pronoun must agree with its antecedent (the noun that the pronoun refers to). *They* and *their* are plural, so the antecedent must also be plural.

The following sentences illustrate the incorrect and the right way to use the pronouns *their* and *they*.

INCORRECT	CORRECT
The artist collected materials for their found-object project.	The artists collected materials for their found-object project.
When a student turns in a late paper, they receive a lower grade.	When students turn in late papers, they receive lower grades.

try this

Have you or your friends coined any new words? What are they? Often, a neologism is also a *portmanteau*, a word that blends two or more words. Staycation is an example of a new word that blended stay at home and vacation. Make up a new word that is also a portmanteau.

Making the antecedent plural isn't always the best solution. Sometimes you want the reader to envision only one individual. In that case, you can use *he* or *she* rather than *they*. Often, it's best just to recast the sentence.

The following sentences illustrate the incorrect usage of the pronoun *they* and ways to rewrite it for a singular antecedent.

INCORRECT	CORRECT	BETTER
A pianist must practice their scales daily.	A pianist must practice his or her scales daily.	A pianist must practice scales daily.

Keep an eye out for other words that are not gender-neutral, such as:

- policeman
- mailman
- chairman
- stewardess
- actress
- man-hours

ADDRESSING PEOPLE AS ONE

When you're addressing people in general, you might be tempted to use the word *one*. For example, *one should avoid sexist language* or *one should mind one's p's and q's*. For Web writing, because you want a more conversational tone, it's best to use *you* when you're speaking about people in general or directly to the reader.

ROMAN NUMERALS

Roman numerals seem to have gone down the path of the buggy whip. No one uses them anymore. When they're used to number chapters in a book or for lists, they make the work seem formal and antiquated. If you use a Roman numeral to represent a number or a date, such as MMX for 2010, you risk being misunderstood by your audience.

Words are the most powerful drug used by mankind.

—Rudyard Kipling

FRENCH AND LATIN PHRASES

Should you use Latin or French phrases in your Web stories? See "Use Foreign Phrases Sparingly" in Chapter 2 to avoid sounding trendy or snooty. If you don't overdo it, a French or Latin phrase can express a sentiment better than the English equivalent.

Grammar Rules

You can't fight it: grammar rules, and if you don't understand the conventions of good grammar, you'd better ask for help. In times when the middle classes are in jeopardy, good grammar is more important than ever. If you don't present yourself well in writing and in speaking, you are perceived as less intelligent and possibly lower class. If you're a job applicant, your cover letter, your emails, and your thank yous need to be letter perfect. Your readers will lose respect for you as an author and distrust your work if it is filled with grammar *faux pas*.

You can stop thinking of the grammarian as the prissy schoolmarm, right now. Grammar is in vogue. (See the sidebar "Grammar is glamour.")

GRAMMAR IS GLAMOUR

Take Our Word For It site authors Melanie and Mike explain how glamour is actually another word for grammar in "What is the origin of the word glamour?" at www.takeourword.com/TOW125/page2.html. Grammar didn't always have such a narrow meaning. Originally, grammar stood for Latin, and grammar school was where you learned Latin grammar. Because church rituals were spoken in Latin, which laypeople didn't understand, they thought those who spoke Latin had special powers, like the priests.

The word grammar evolved to have two meanings. In the Middle Ages, the English word *gramarye* stood for the rules for sentence structure and knowledge of the occult. The French word *gramaire* evolved to the modern French term *grimoire*, which is a textbook of magic. *Glamour*, the Scottish version of *grammar*, evolved to mean a spell that caused an altered vision of reality. The meaning of glamour shifted again to mean magical beauty and then eventually evolved to the definition you use today. Dust off your grammar books! There's still a lot of magic to be learned from them.

The Grammar Police

You're probably already aware of the grammar police. They lurk by the side of the Web highway with radar guns, watching for reckless endangerment of the English language. Did you speed through more than one sentence without coming to a full stop? If you're pulled over for questioning, will you be able to defend yourself? The grammar police can be forceful, but if you learn a few basics, you'll be in the clear. Arm yourself with a good grammar source, so when the grammar police threaten to take you in, you can question their authority.

Here are a couple of terrific online grammar resources:

- The Purdue Online Writing Lab (OWL) at http://owl.english.purdue.edu
- Grammar Girl, Quick and Dirty Tips at http://grammar.quickanddirtytips.com

When Can You Ignore the Rules?

Just as the English language is continually evolving, so are the rules of grammar. If you are a baby boomer or belong to an earlier generation, you learned the following three rules in grade school:

1. **Never end a sentence with a preposition. For example, don't write:**
   Where are you from?
2. **Never split an infinitive, such as to go. For example, don't write:**
   To boldly go where no man has gone before.
3. **Always write complete sentences. For example, don't write:**
   Enjoying the rain.

These days, many professional writers, including baby boomers, intentionally ignore these three rules without losing the respect of their readership. So, when can you ignore the rules? You can disregard them only when you can get away with it. If you don't understand the rules and you're careless with your sentence formation, the grammar police will be on high alert and pay you a visit.

To make fun of the rule prohibiting you from ending a sentence with a proposition, Winston Churchill said, "That is something up with which I will not put." George Orwell offers some good advice in his essay "Politics and the English Language." Orwell claims that six rules cover most cases. The last one is to "Break any of these rules sooner than say anything outright barbarous." You can read the full essay at http://orwell.ru/library/essays/politics/english/e_polit.

Common Grammar Errors

The following sections describe some of the most common grammatical errors. Your readers might find these errors egregious, but they are easy to avoid.

APOSTROPHES

One of the most common grammatical errors is to use an apostrophe where it doesn't belong or to leave one out when it does belong. Two words that fall into this category are *its* and *it's*. The first, *its*, is a possessive pronoun, and because it's possessive, some writers think it needs an apostrophe. But possessive pronouns (mine, yours, his, hers, ours, theirs) show ownership without the apostrophe. The word *it's* is a contraction for it is. In this case, only use an apostrophe if the word stands for it is.

It's = it is

The following sentences illustrate incorrect and correct usage of it's and its.

INCORRECT	CORRECT
Its sad to be all alone in the world.	It's sad to be all alone in the world.

You're = you are

Another common error is to use the word your when you mean you're. The same rule applies here. *You're* is a contraction of the words you are. *Your* is a possessive pronoun and doesn't take an apostrophe.

Another common error is the plural form of acronyms and dates with an apostrophe. For example, the plural of CD is CDs, not CD's.

The following illustrates incorrect and correct usage for plural dates and acronyms.

INCORRECT	CORRECT
1960's	1960s
DVD's	DVDs

ME OR I?

Is it me or I? Many writers get confused by these simple pronouns. Look at the following sentence: *Sally and me went to the movies.* It sounds OK, and you hear lots of other people using me rather than I in sentences with similar syntax. However, it's wrong. In this case, it should be I, because I is the subject.

INCORRECT	CORRECT
Sally and me went to the movies.	Sally and I went to the movies.

Some authors have been corrected so many times on such sentences that they overcorrect when I is at the end of the sentence; for example, in the sentence *Mom baked a cake for Jeff and I.* In this case, I is not correct, because it's no longer the subject of the sentence. Mom is the subject.

INCORRECT	CORRECT
Mom baked a cake for Jeff and I.	Mom baked a cake for Jeff and me.

An easy way tell whether to use me or I correctly in your sentences is to cross out the other person in the sentence. You can then better tell by the sound of the sentence if it's correct. In each of the sentences in **FIGURE 8.1**, you can more easily hear that me and I are not correct when the second person is crossed out.

The misuse of language induces evil in the soul.

—Socrates

 *~~Mary and~~ me went to the movies.*

Mom baked a cake for ~~Jeff and~~ I.

FIGURE 8.1
Incorrect pronouns don't sound right on their own.

Malapropisms

It's funny to hear someone else say the wrong word, but it's not fun when you're the target of the laughter. Be a lifelong learner of the English language and continue to build your vocabulary. Keep a notebook of new words you've learned and those that you've misused in the past. If you're not confident about the following terms that are often erroneously interchanged, look up their meanings in your favorite online dictionary:

- Affect versus effect
- Principle versus principal
- Discrete versus discreet
- Alright versus all right
- Everytime versus every time

Literally is a word that you'll hear misused almost daily. When something literally occurs, it's a fact that it occurs. The antonym is figurative. A figure of speech is symbolic and more imaginative. If you hear someone say, for example, "She charmed the pants off me, literally," it means that that person was no longer wearing his pants.

 try this

Listen carefully to any spoken words for an entire day. Note words that aren't used correctly.

Mouses or Mice

If you're talking about a small furry rodent, you know that one such creature is called a mouse and several are called mice. But what about the pointing device that works with your laptop? One is called a mouse, but if you have more than one, do you call them mice or mouses? Some readers will cringe when they see mouses. However, there is a large population in India that uses mouses for the plural of the pointing devices. The English language often accommodates what the majority speaks, so it may be that in the future, mouses will be considered correct. At this point, it still hasn't been decided, so it's a style choice for you to make.

Spelling Mnemonics

If spelling doesn't come easily for you, make sure you use a spell checker and a reliable dictionary. Do not try to use a search engine to discover the correct spelling for a word. You're likely to find several instances of the word misspelled. For example, if you Google *accomodate* rather than *accommodate*, you'll find it again and again, misspelled.

Mnemonics can help jog your memory for certain words that are often misspelled.

The following examples show words that are easy to misspell and their helpful mnemonics.

WORD	MNEMONIC
Misspell	Begins with the word miss. A near miss?
Separate	There's "a rat" in separate
Dessert	Has a double s for strawberry shortcake
Entomology	Has three Os. When you put them together (ooo) they look like the three characteristic body parts for insects: the head, the thorax, and the abdomen.

Punctuation

Write the following sentence putting in the correct punctuation.

WOMAN WITHOUT HER MAN IS NOTHING

Can you see how the meaning can radically change depending on how you add commas or exclamation points? In your sentence was the woman or the man nothing?

Getting all your commas, apostrophes, quotation marks, and so forth in the right place can be tiresome. But without strictly adhering to convention, your Web content will not be clear.

Some individuals are passionate about preserving language conventions and will go to great lengths to correct errors. See the sidebar "Typo Vigilantes."

TYPO VIGILANTES

CBS Sunday Morning correspondent Bill Geist interviewed Jeff Deck and Benjamin Herson, whose mission is to wipe out typos and grammar errors on American signs (www.cbsnews.com/video/watch/?id=6944729n). In 2008, Deck and Herson took a road trip to correct as many typos as they could find on behalf of their organization, Typo Eradication Advancement League (TEAL). They did not know that one of the signs they fixed on the Grand Canyon's South Rim was listed as a national landmark. Deck and Herson were fined $3000 and banned from public parks for a year. They've learned from their naiveté and now ask for permission before pulling out their sign-correction tools.

Challenges

The best way to get better at writing Web content is to write, write some more, and rewrite. The challenges in this chapter focus on style and grammar.

Freewriting

The freewriting challenges in this chapter ask you to practice writing with style and grammar in mind.

Freewriting works best when it is timed. If you tend to write quickly, set the timer for ten minutes. If you tend to take a little more time, give yourself 15 minutes. Remember that with freewriting you don't need to worry about accuracy, grammar, spelling, and so forth.

WHAT ANNOYS ME

Do you have a pet peeve regarding style or grammar? What is it? Write a paragraph to explain why it annoys you.

MY PERSONAL STYLE

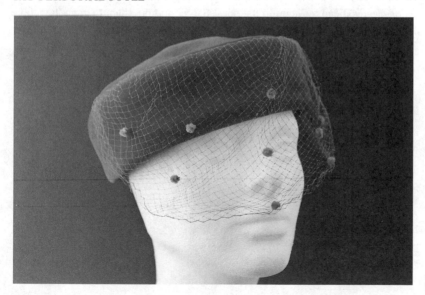

Write a paragraph that describes the style you like best. Explain whether it's more formal or casual. Do you use foreign phrases? Who is the audience?

Suggested Exercises

Exercises are longer projects that will take more time to complete. You can find more complete instructions, learning outcomes, and criteria for critiquing your work at www.write4web.com.

A RULE I INTENTIONALLY BREAK

Is there a grammar rule that you cannot abide by? What is it, and how do you justify not adhering to its convention?

NETIQUETTE

Develop a set of rules for Internet etiquette. What are good policies? What should be avoided? For example, one of your rules might be to not disclose everyone's email on a distribution list. Private information, such as telephone numbers, should also not be disclosed. For this exercise, collaboration works well.

Up Next

Now that you've considered your own style and reviewed a few grammatical guidelines, you can move on to the next chapter and put them to use. Chapter 9, "Telling a Good Story," discusses the elements of good storytelling and how stories satisfy deep cravings.

9

Telling a Good Story

Once upon a time—these few words can stop a frustrated child from screaming, prevent an unruly group of students from creating havoc, and change an entire nation's perspective. Humans are hard-wired for storytelling, spending much of their waking time engrossed In stories, including those on the Web and in books, movies, games, radio programs, business presentations, speeches, and casual conversations.

Whether you are writing fiction or nonfiction, the ability to tell a good story is a skill you want to cultivate. This chapter explores:

- What makes a good story
- Refining your senses
- Starting stories with a hook
- Structuring your story

What Makes a Good Story?

Ask 100 people what makes a good story, and you'll get 100 different answers. Some are drawn to stories that are character driven, and some love fast-action, plot-driven stories. Some enjoy coming-of-age tales, or *bildungsroman*. Some enjoy adventures. Some love to watch movies set in cities they've visited, such as London, Paris, Florence, Tokyo, or Nairobi. Some love film noir, some love love stories, and some love comedies.

try this

Do you like character-driven or plot-driven stories? List the last five movies that you've enjoyed. What did you like about them? The plot? The setting? The characters? Write down three things you liked about each film.

Fiction writer Eudora Welty said that place is everything. In Welty's story "Why I Live at the P.O.," the setting becomes a main character in the story. You can hear it in the dialogue, and the entire short story answers the dramatic question of why the main narrator, called Sister, ends up living at the post office. For those who love Eudora Welty, the setting and the world the characters inhabit are what make it a good story.

Aristotle said that plot (he called it mythos) was the most important element in a story. He believed that all the trials and tribulations the character withstood took second place to the events of the story. If you like mysteries and action adventure, you probably like plot-driven stories.

If you like Quentin Tarantino films, you probably like character-driven stories. *Pulp Fiction* unfolds the stories of several characters in a nonlinear sequence with rich dialogue that makes the characters believable and endearing.

Good storytellers can charm, soothe, placate, heal, educate, warn, and incite their audience to action.

IMAGINATION

According to Paul Bloom, you spend more time in fictional worlds than anywhere else. He reports in "The Pleasures of Imagination" (http://chronicle.com/article/The-Pleasures-of-Imagination/65678) that when "we are free to do whatever we want, we retreat to the imagination—to worlds created by others, as with books, movies, video games, and television (over four hours a day for the average American), or to worlds we ourselves create, as when daydreaming and fantasizing." How do you spend your free time?

Story Elements

Stories don't feel complete if they are missing important elements. For example, you might have the most fascinating characters, but if there's no conflict and your main character doesn't seem to want anything, your readers will feel the story is too long, pointless, and boring. If the setting feels hazy, it's hard to develop the characters as sympathetic and believable. Regardless of whether the story is character driven or plot driven, you need to build other elements into your story.

The following list provides a brief review of the elements of a story and the questions they answer:

- **Characters.** Who is the story about?
- **Conflict.** What is the problem?
- **Place.** Where does the story take place?
- **Plot.** What happens to the characters?
- **Premise.** What's the main idea or focus of the story?
- **Backstory.** What happens before the story begins?
- **Theme.** What is the universal condition in the story? Think big picture for this one, such as *the human condition*, or *humans against nature* or *humans against humans*.
- **Tone.** What is the attitude and atmosphere of the story? A story's tone might be sardonic, funny, lighthearted, heavy, sad, angry, or defensive.

try this

Choose one of the following traditional story beginnings and see where it leads you:

- Once upon a time
- Long ago, in a faraway land
- It all began when
- In the beginning
- I'll tell you a story

PLOT VS. STORY

What is the difference between plot and story? In *Aspects of the Novel* (Mariner Books, 1956), E.M. Forster explains how plot differs from story. "'The King died and then the Queen died' is a story. 'The King died, and then the Queen died of grief' is a plot." A story is a narrative that describes the events that occur within the story's time frame. A plot is also a narrative, describing the events that occur, but with causality. With the King and Queen, the story describes what happened to the King and Queen. The plot explains what happened and why the Queen died.

Developing Stories

There's no one way to structure a story, and much of how you structure yours will depend on the story you want to tell. However, this section includes a few helpful guidelines.

A classic way to tell a story is to begin with a problem or a character's deep desire. Then continue the story with a series of escalating events whereby the problem is either solved or not solved, or the character obtains or does not obtain the desire. These events culminate at the climax of the story, at which point the action has escalated as far as it can go. Then finish the story with how the character responds to the outcome of events. Sometimes everyone lives happily ever after, and sometimes everyone dies.

Tell me a fact and I'll learn. Tell me a truth and I'll believe. But tell me a story and it will live in my heart forever.

—Indian proverb

What's your story? If someone asks what you've been up to, what do you say? Write a few lines that describe your current circumstances.

Here are a few other suggestions for structuring a story:

- **Include a beginning, middle, and end.** According to Aristotle, a story needs a beginning, middle, and end.

- **Begin in the middle.** Start at an exciting point in the story. See the section "Jump In" later in this chapter for more information.

- **Begin with a problem.** Describe at the outset what the character dearly wants or what trouble the character is having.

- **Tell how the trouble escalates.** In the middle of the story, describe how the characters cope with the problem or reach for their desires.

- **Sprinkle gold coins throughout the story.** Make sure you add a bit of excitement or some juicy details every so often within the story to hold your readers' interest. For example, if your character is destitute, on the streets, starving, and bedraggled, don't continue page after page after page without a small gleam of hope or a humorous moment in the character's existence.

If your story unfolds like a mystery, you might follow the organization of a traditional crime novel: Begin by announcing the mystery; then parade all the suspects through; throw readers off by making them think an innocent person committed the crime; and then end the story by solving the crime and capturing the true perpetrator.

Refine Your Senses

Humans prize their stereoscopic vision; however, while you're writing, don't forget to describe with all your senses. Use visual details to paint vivid pictures. Add gustatory, olfactory, tactile, and auditory details to draw your readers completely into the story.

SENSAZIONE

Michael Gelb reveals in *How to Think Like Leonardo da Vinci* (Delacorte, 1998) that da Vinci felt developing the senses was an important part of fully realizing experiences. Sensazione is defined as "the continual refinement of the senses, especially sight, as a means to enliven experience." One of da Vinci's mottos was *saper vedere*, or knowing how to see. You can develop your sensory experiences with active and focused seeing, smelling, tasting, and touching.

As an author, you'll want to refine your senses and your vocabulary to describe the senses. Try to make your own lists of words to describe smells, sounds, and so forth for individual topics that you write about. If you write about artisan breads, for example, your vocabulary list for textures might include words such as crispy, crunchy, smooth, and dense. If you write about coffees, your vocabu-lary for tastes might include words such as dark roast, full-bodied, acidic, and nutty. Sometimes it's hard to think of exactly the right word to define a smell or taste. Use the following lists to jog your memory for descriptive adjectives:

- **Words to describe smells.** Acidic, acrid, aromatic, camphoric, fetid, fragrant, fresh, musky, musty, piney, pungent, rancid, savory

- **Words to describe sounds.** Bang, blare, chime, chirp, crunch, drone, fizz, grind, groan, gulp, gurgle, hoot, howl, jangle, knock, ping, plop, rap, rattle, roar, rumble, rustle, sizzle, slam, slap, strum, tap, thud, whine, whistle

- **Words to describe tastes.** Acidic, biting, bitter, briny, dry, fruity, full-bodied, gamy, peppery, rich, sharp, sour, sugary, sweet, tangy, tart, zesty, zingy

- **Words to describe touch.** Bristly, burning, cold, damp, dry, feathery, frosty, furry, fuzzy, gnarled, hairy, hot, knotted, leathery, limp, lumpy, rough, rub-bery, sandy, sharp, slimy, smooth, sticky, velvety

SYNESTHESIA

The literary term *synesthesia* means to blend the senses. For example, you might describe a sound with color or a color with scent. Describing snow as cool and white or the sun as blaring red are examples of synesthesia. You can find examples of this technique in literature throughout the ages, especially in English romantic poetry and Japanese postmodern novels. Read *Snow Country* by Nobel Prize winner Yasunari Kawabata for beauti-ful, lyrical impressions and plenty of examples of synesthesia.

Explore in ways you never have. Close your eyes while you're listening to Mozart. Try wine tasting while blindfolded. Compare textures with scents. Wear sunglasses at night and walk through your neighborhood. Smell a bouquet of fresh flowers and describe the blended scents.

Jump In

Novice writers sometimes think they must begin a story at the chronologi-cal beginning. This is a big mistake. The best place to start a story is to jump right into the middle of the action. This is the advice Aristotle gave, calling it *in media res,* which means into the middle of things.

Let's consider the first sentence of *Oliver Twist* by Charles Dickens:

Among other public buildings in a certain town, which for many reasons it will be prudent to refrain from mentioning, and to which I will assign no fic-titious name, there is one anciently common to most towns, great or small: to wit, a workhouse; and in this workhouse was born; on a day and date which I need not trouble myself to repeat, inasmuch as it can be of no pos-sible consequence to the reader, in this stage of the business at all events; the item of mortality whose name is prefixed to the head of this chapter.

Most creative writing teachers will tell you not to start your story with "It was a dark and stormy night" because this phrase is a cliché. However, Madeleine L'Engle won a Newberry Medal for her children's book *A Wrinkle in Time*, which begins with this phrase. Try beginning a fictional story with this cliché or another that you like.

Go to your favorite bookstore and read the first few lines of the current bestsellers. What techniques do you find? Which hooks made you want to buy the book?

try this

Pause for a moment and recall your favorite TV shows or movies. How do they begin? What techniques are used to hook you? The next time you're on the Internet, pay attention to the beginnings of stories. What hooks are employed?

This initial sentence, besides being way too long, starts with the birth of the main character, Oliver. But today's readers don't want a lengthy beginning. For a modern story, it is best to jump in and begin the story after Oliver has fled from Mr. Bumble and the funeral business, walked 70 miles to London, and met the Artful Dodger. Once the audience is immersed in Oliver's struggles in London, the author could then relate details about Oliver's birth and how he got to London with backstory.

Start with a Hook

It was a dark and stormy night...

To obtain your reader's full attention, not only do you need to start the story in the middle at an exciting moment, but you need to start with a hook. Good hooks, the first one or two sentences that begin your story, will grab readers and make them want to read more. Readers often decide whether or not they will continue reading a story based on the first three sentences.

Write your beginning sentences with the following goals in mind:

- Start the story
- Set the tone
- Introduce major characters
- Create curiosity
- Pose the dramatic question that the story must answer (begin the conflict)

A Web site's home page has the same goals—to hook viewers, lure them into the site, and make them want to return again and again.

The next few sections contain some techniques for writing good hooks. The hook you write might employ more than one of these techniques. But don't limit yourself to the ideas presented here.

A Gripping Event

Start the story with an event that demands your readers' attention.

Here are a few examples:

- **From Milan Kundera's *The Book of Laughter and Forgetting*.** "In February 1948, Communist leader Klement Gottwald stepped out on the balcony of a Baroque palace in Prague to address the hundreds of thousands of his fellow citizens packed into Old Town Square. It was a crucial moment in Czech history—a fateful moment of the kind that occurs once or twice in a millennium."
- **From John Updike's short story "A&P."** "In walks these girls in nothing but bathing suits."

A Memorable Character

Start the story with an unusual character. There's a great example, both in film and in literature. Kids young and old love the animated *Shrek* movies. If you haven't yet read the children's book the movies are based on, you're in for a treat. William Steig wrote *Shrek!* in 1990. It begins with a picture of the young ogre, cute in a gruesome way, at his birthplace. The first two sentences read:

> His mother was ugly and his father was ugly, but Shrek was uglier than the two of them put together. By the time he toddled, Shrek could spit flame a full ninety-nine yards and vent smoke from ear to ear.

Here are more examples:

- **From J. R. R. Tolkien's *Lord of the Rings.*** "When Mr. Bilbo Baggins of Bag End announced that he would shortly be celebrating his eleventy-first birthday with a party of special magnificence, there was much talk and excitement in Hobbiton."
- **From Roald Dahl's *Matilda.*** "It's a funny thing about mothers and fathers. Even when their own child is the most disgusting little blister you could ever imagine, they still think that he or she is wonderful."

> *Those who do not have power over the story that dominates their lives, the power to retell it, rethink it, deconstruct it, joke about it, and change it as times change, truly are powerless, because they cannot think new thoughts.*
>
> —Salman Rushdie

A Strange Incident

Start the story with an unusual incident or strange circumstance. This technique is popular with TV crime shows.

Here are a few examples:

- **From Ambrose Bierce's "An Occurrence at Owl Creek Bridge.** "A man stood upon a railroad bridge in northern Alabama, looking down into the swift water twenty feet below. The man's hands were behind his back, the wrists bound with a cord. A rope closely encircled his neck."
- **From George Orwell's *1984.*** "It was a bright cold day in April, and the clocks were striking thirteen."

Rich Setting

Start the story with a flamboyant setting or rich atmosphere.

Here are a few examples:

- **From Xinran Xinran's *Sky Burial.*** "Her inscrutable eyes looked past me at the world outside the window—the crowded street, the noisy traffic, the regimented lines of tower blocks."

- **From Lesley M.M. Blume's *Cornelia and the Audacious Escapades of the Somerset Sisters.*** "It was winter in New York City and the days were short. At three o'clock in the afternoon, the sun already hung low over the horizon, casting sharp pink light on the clouds above the skyscrapers."

Character in Big Trouble

Start the story with a character in jeopardy. The film *The Fugitive* is a good example: It begins with the police questioning Dr. Richard Kimble, whose wife has just been murdered. You quickly learn that the police suspect Kimble has killed his wife.

Here are more examples:

- **From Janice Steinberg's *Death in a City of Mystics.*** "The snakes! Didn't anyone warn them about the snakes?"
- **From Edgar Allan Poe's "The Tell-Tale Heart."** "TRUE!—nervous—very, very dreadfully nervous I had been and am; but why will you say that I am mad? The disease had sharpened my senses—not destroyed—not dulled them."

Beautiful Language

Start the story with exciting language.

Here are a few examples:

- **From Sue Monk Kidd's *The Secret Life of Bees.*** "At night I would lie in bed and watch the show, how bees squeezed through the cracks of my bedroom wall and flew circles around the room, making that propeller sound, a high-pitched zzzzzz that hummed along my skin."
- **From Alice Walker's *The Color Purple.*** "You better not never tell nobody but God."

Add Cliff-hangers

For episodic stories, cliff-hangers ensure that your readers will want to continue to the next story in the series. A cliff-hanger concludes a single episode with the character in dire trouble, perhaps dangling off a cliff, and then suddenly ends. The audience doesn't know if the character will be saved or fall to a harrowing death and has to continue with the next episode to find out. If you follow any TV shows, you're well aware of how a cliff-hanger works. At the end of the season, the main character might even appear to have been killed. Then, miraculously, at the beginning of the new season, the character is still alive and continues with the show.

STORY-DELAYING

In his beautifully illustrated book, *Directing the Story* (Focal Press, 2009), story artist Francis Glebas explains that the secret of storytelling is story-delaying. His book illustrates how a professional creates storyboards, and he shows how to illustrate using the story line of *The Arabian Nights: Tales from One Thousand and One Nights*.

The story *The Arabian Nights* is a frame story, meaning there is a story within the story. The first story tells of the courage of Scheherazade, a brave young woman who has decided to marry a terrible Sultan in spite of the consequences. The Sultan, having been betrayed by his first wife, each night takes a new bride and then has her killed the following morning to avoid another betrayal. Scheherazade has a plan, which she shares with her beloved sister Dinarzade. On the wedding night, Scheherazade asks if she might spend some time with her sister Dinarzade and bid her farewell. According to the plan, Dinarzade asks Scheherazade to tell her one last story. Then the internal story begins. Scheherazade begins the tale of the first night and stops right at the cliff-hanger. The Sultan, naturally, wants to know what happens next. Scheherazade yawns and says there's not enough time to finish. To find out how the story ends, the Sultan spares her life for another day. The second night, a new story begins, and again leaves off in the middle at an exciting cliff-hanger. The next day Scheherazade's life is spared again. The stories continue for 1000 more nights, and by that time the Sultan has fallen in love with Scheherazade.

Challenges

The best way to get better at writing Web content is to write, write some more, and rewrite. The challenges in this chapter focus on refining your senses and storytelling techniques.

Freewriting

The freewriting challenges in this chapter ask you to practice writing with storytelling in mind.

Freewriting works best when it is timed. If you tend to write quickly, set the timer for ten minutes. If you tend to take a little more time, give yourself 15 minutes. Remember that with freewriting you don't need to worry about accuracy, grammar, spelling, and so forth.

CHOCOLATE

This practice requires a piece of chocolate. (If you don't eat chocolate, a banana works well.) Slowly open your chocolate. Listen to the sound of the wrapper. Describe how the wrapper looks and feels. Describe the taste, the smell, and the touch of the chocolate (or banana). Take your time.

WRITE A HOOK

Write a hook for Web content you are currently writing or about to write. Using one of the suggested methods in this chapter, write a hook for the story.

Suggested Exercise

Exercises are longer projects that will take more time to complete. You can find more complete instructions, learning outcomes, and criteria for critiquing your work at www.write4web.com.

SHORT STORY

Write a short short story or an anecdote (less than 1000 words) that follows a classic story structure.

Up Next

With the knowledge that your best Web content will tell a good story, you can move on to Chapter 10. Chapter 10 offers an irreverent guide to Aristotle's principles and a review of rhetorical modes.

10

A Refresher on the Rhetorical Modes

If you've taken a class on writing college papers or public speaking, you're already familiar with the rhetorical modes. The principles of rhetoric started with the Ancient Greeks and have been handed down through the ages. How can this ancient knowledge improve your Web content? Keep reading to discover how the age-old strategies, patterns, and guidelines for rhetoric, with a few changes to adapt to modern audiences, can give your Web content clarity, spark, and meaning. This chapter covers:

- A review of the rhetorical modes
- Making Web content credible
- Finding a pattern for your story
- Persuading with images

Rhetorical Modes

Rhetorical modes offer effective patterns for organizing your thoughts and putting them down on paper. The four traditional modes include:

- **Narration.** Tells what happened.
- **Description.** Presents a picture of what happened.
- **Explanation.** Makes what happened more understandable.
- **Argument.** Persuades you to agree or disagree with what happened.

I write to discover what I know.

—Flannery O'Connor

While you are composing, there's no need to try to isolate which mode you will work in. Most stories cross boundaries, perhaps beginning with narration and then slipping into an argument that involves description and explanation. Practicing the modes separately, however, can hone your writing skills.

The following sections describe in more detail each of the rhetorical modes.

Narration

Narration tells a story by walking the reader through a series of events. The thesis for narration is implied and often expressed as a mood, attitude, or impression. This mode is organized chronologically and answers some or all of the following questions:

- Who is involved?
- What happened?
- Where did it happen?
- When did it happen?
- How did it happen?
- Why did it happen?

The narrative mode is predominantly used for Web content such as biographies, reflections, oral histories, and interviews. Most Web content includes some narration, whether it's a short anecdote, a paragraph recounting the history of a topic, or several pages of a personal account that form part of a longer story, such as a case study.

Description

Description shows a picture of someone or something. Description works best when you provide vivid significant details and draw readers in with impressions from all of your senses. This mode is organized by emphasis or spatially and answers questions about how the topic looks, feels, tastes, smells, and sounds. Description is predominantly used in product descriptions, but all Web content needs descriptive details to make the story come to life.

Explanation

Explanatory (also called expository) composition informs readers with explanations, definitions, examples, comparisons, and more. When your story fits this mode, don't be afraid to format most of the story with lists, which are easy to read. You can find a good example of the explanatory mode, presented mostly with bullet points, on Holland's Web site at www.holland.com/global/Tourism/Holland-information/About-Holland/Did-you-know.htm?alt=Did%20you%20know%3F. The page titled Did You Know offers a variety of curious facts and anecdotes about the country.

The explanatory mode is a broad category that includes several subgenres— a few of which are discussed in the following sections.

PROCESS OR INSTRUCTION

A process or instruction tells readers how something works, usually in chronological order. Because this subgenre is prevalent on the Web and important, Chapter 11, "Writing Instructions," is devoted to this topic.

CLASSIFICATION AND DIVISION

Classification groups objects or ideas into large classes or categories. Division breaks down objects or ideas into smaller parts.

COMPARE AND CONTRAST

Compare and contrast stories point out similarities and differences, typically for two or three objects. There are two classic organizational patterns: Either each object is presented fully, one at a time, or the objects are examined point by point. The point-by-point organization is often easier to manage for Web content and allows you to compose with shorter paragraphs.

Compare and contrast stories typically involve a learning process. You share information with your readers that you discovered while probing and analyzing the subjects.

> *Over time and cultures, the most robust and most effective form of communication is the creation of a powerful narrative.*
>
> —Howard Gardner

CAUSE AND EFFECT

Cause and effect stories explain either the reasons something occurred (the causes) or explain a situation and describe the effects. In many cases there are multiple causes or multiple effects. When writing a story where one thing causes an effect, and then that effect causes another effect, and so on, the organization is called a domino effect. For example, fossil carbon emissions cause the Greenhouse Effect. This causes climate change, which causes the Earth's polar ice caps to melt, causing sea levels to rise.

PROBLEM AND SOLUTION

The problem and solution type of Web content informs readers about possible problems and suggests ways to solve or mitigate the problem. This mode works well for Frequently Asked Questions (FAQs) to help readers easily find answers for common issues.

Argument

Using the argument mode, you take a position that is somewhat controversial and then provide valid reasons to support that position in hopes of persuading your readers to join your side of the debate.

Rhetoric in Ancient Greece

Rhetoric has been taught in English classes for centuries and is based on Aristotelian principles set forth in his writings. The word *rhetoric* today refers to the spoken and the written word, but in Ancient Greece, the term *rhetorikós* applied to oration, or the art of public speaking. Aristotle described rhetoric as the art of persuasion. According to Aristotle (see the sidebar "Aristotle and His Teacher, Plato"), the three ways to persuade your audience were by appealing to:

Write "I have three passions." List what they are and add a few details about each. Describe, in one sentence, why you feel passionate about each. What would you say to someone else to persuade that person to share your passion?

- **Ethos, or moral character.** The audience is persuaded by the speaker's sense of honesty and integrity. The speaker appeals to the reader's conscience, ethics, morals, standards, values, and principles.
- **Pathos, or emotions.** The audience is persuaded by its passions and deep beliefs. The speaker appeals to the reader's heart, emotions, sympathies, and sentimentalities.
- **Logos, or logic.** The audience is persuaded by its sense of logic. The speaker appeals to the reader's intellect using logic, numbers, explanations, and facts.

These three methods of persuasion influence modern readers. Your content must appeal to ethos or be deemed credible, as discussed in the next section. When you take a stance and argue a position with examples and reasoning that appeal to your readers' hearts and minds, or pathos and logos, you're more likely to win their support for your cause or belief. And if you don't win them over, you'll at the very least gain their respect.

ARISTOTLE AND HIS TEACHER, PLATO

In *Rhetoric* (translated by W. Rhys Roberts), Aristotle explains that there are three divisions of rhetoric: political, forensic, and ceremonial. (See Book I, Part 3 at http://classics.mit.edu/Aristotle/rhetoric.1.i.html.) Political speeches urge listeners to take action or not take action; forensic speeches either attack or defend someone; and ceremonial speeches praise or blame someone. Aristotle also links each type of speech to time. Political rhetoric is for the future; forensic is for the past; and ceremonial is for the present.

Aristotle's teacher, Plato, wasn't convinced that writing was a good invention. Before the written word, songs and stories were passed down from ancestors orally. In the introduction to *Committed to Memory: 100 Best Poems to Memorize* (Turtle Point, 2000), editor John Hollander mentions a story in Plato's *Phaedrus* where Socrates talks about the Egyptian gods Thoth and Ammon. When Thoth shows his written characters to Ammon, Ammon scolds him saying, "This discovery of yours will create forgetfulness in the learners' souls, because they will not use their memories. They will trust to the external written characters and not remember themselves."

Can you imagine a world without writing?

You can read Plato's *Phaedrus* online at http://classics.mit.edu/Plato/phaedrus.html.

Making Web Content Credible

Have you heard about dihydrogen monoxide (DHMO), also called dihydrogen oxide? DHMO is a colorless and odorless chemical compound that:

- Causes severe tissue damage with prolonged exposure.
- Results in death with accidental inhalation, even in small doses.
- Is found in biopsies of precancerous tumors and lesions.

The Dihydrogen Monoxide Research Division offers more information, including *special reports*, about this controversial substance at www.dhmo.org. Scared?

Before you jump to a hasty conclusion and decide to ban DHMO, make sure your information is accurate and comes from a credible source. Search for DHMO on the Web and read at least two more articles. You'll soon discover that the DHMO site is a hoax. The main purpose of the Dihydrogen Monoxide Research Division is to show you that information on the Web that seems true because it is couched in scientific jargon can be complete nonsense.

To maintain your readers' trust that you are a credible source of information, you must spend time on due diligence to ascertain the truth of factual information you present. Keep Aristotle's ethos in mind as you research information. You want your readers to believe that you are an author of good character, that you make a stalwart effort to speak the truth, and that you back up your claims with valid facts from credible sources.

Here are a few more guidelines to ensure that your audience finds your work credible:

What characteristics of Web content make you suspicious? What makes you doubt the credibility of a Web site? Make a few notes about anything that you've seen on the Web that has made you wary.

- Avoid errors. Even a typo can mar your readers' opinion of you as an author. If you do make a factual mistake or even a typo, correct it.
- Avoid generalizations and off-the-cuff remarks.
- Keep your messages clear, direct, and straightforward.
- Don't include obvious promotional content or ads.
- Provide a short bio that describes your expertise.
- Provide a way for readers to contact you.
- Offer citations, references, and source materials so readers can verify information that you provide.

Rhetoric for Web Content

Aristotle offered some great advice on how to reach an audience, but it's time to update some of his teachings and principles. If you've read any translations of Plato or Aristotle's writings, you'll agree that the Greeks could have improved their own writings with a few of the techniques discussed in this book, such as:

- Use the inverted pyramid style.
- Use titles and subtitles.
- Use numbered and bulleted lists.
- Keep sentences and paragraphs short.
- Stick to one topic per paragraph.

Patterns and Strategies

Every Web story has a unique structure and pattern of development, depending on its content, and there's no one-size-fits-all organization. However, parts of your story, if well written, will fit the traditional patterns and guidelines suggested by the Ancient Greeks.

One of the first decisions you need to make is to choose the point of view for telling the story.

Point of View

The point of view for your story can be first person, second person, or third person. It's important not to mix and match point of view, but rather to use one consistently. When choosing a point of view, consider the following:

- **First person.** For example: *I don't like going to movies at the theater, especially because the tickets are so expensive.* This perspective works well when the story includes personal experiences, observations, and reflections. With first person, you tell the story as the narrator using the pronouns I, me, mine, we, our, and us. If you don't want the content to feel subjective, choose another point of view.

- **Second person.** For example: *You pay dearly to see a movie at the theatre, but is it worth it?* This perspective works especially well for giving instructions or explanations. With second person, you speak directly to the reader using the pronoun you.

- **Third person.** For example: *Watching movies at the theater is an expensive and often frustrating endeavor.* This perspective works well for general reporting and content that you want to feel more objective. With third person, you don't refer to either the reader or you as the writer. You use the pronouns he, she, their, them, and they.

Review the first paragraph of any story that you have already written. What point of view did you choose? Did that point of view work well? Try rewriting the story using a different point of view. Notice how the story changes and whether or not you like the changes.

Beginnings, Middles, and Endings

Aristotle believed that every story needed a beginning, middle, and end. For a traditional college paper that follows Aristotelian principles, the classic structure has five paragraphs or more:

- Paragraph 1 introduces the topic with a general statement. The next several sentences build up to the thesis statement, which is at the end of the paragraph.

- Paragraphs 2–4 (or more) support the thesis statement with anecdotes, examples, and facts.

- Paragraph 5 (or the last paragraph) concludes the essay.

This structure, which is prescribed by many college texts, uses a pyramid style of organization for paragraphs and the entire essay. According to Aristotle, when providing examples to support a thesis, it's best to save the most important and best example for last.

However, for Web writing, it's best to use the inverted pyramid style for individual paragraphs as well as the entire essay. (The inverted pyramid style for paragraphs is discussed in Chapter 2, "Best Practices for Writing for the Web.") With the inverted pyramid style, the first paragraph of the story begins with the most important sentence, the thesis statement, and ends with the least important sentence. In the same vein, the entire essay is organized with the most important information first followed by supporting examples and facts of lesser and lesser importance.

Thesis or Topic Sentences

The thesis is the main point or purpose of your composition. For fictional stories and nonfictional narrative, the thesis is implied and often not overtly stated. For all other types of stories, without a clearly stated thesis, you will have trouble pulling together a cohesive story. The body of your story exists to support the thesis, but if there is no thesis or the thesis is vague, too broad, or too narrow, you will have trouble organizing clear and cohesive paragraphs, and the composition, as a whole, will feel disjointed.

A good thesis sentence makes a statement and shows the author's perspective about that statement. Mere observations or announcements do not work as thesis statements.

The following sentences illustrate good thesis statements as well as those that won't provide a strong enough basis for a story.

GOOD THESIS	MERE OBSERVATION
If parents better understood ESRB video game ratings, fewer children would be exposed to games designed for mature players.	Video games are rated by the Entertainment Software Rating Board (ESRB).

TOO BROAD	TOO NARROW
Teens play a lot of video games.	Video games are now portable.

Common Structural Problems

Even if you have a clear, strong thesis, your Web story can lose its tension because the structure is weak or the pattern doesn't fit the content. Here are a few problems to avoid:

- **Flashbacks or flash forwards in time.** Keep in mind that with Web content, the reader has a harder time following the story if you make extensive use of flashbacks and backstory. With narration, try to tell the story chronologically.
- **Effusive description.** Readers don't want to be deluged with details. Keep the story succinct and vivid.
- **Missing information.** Especially when explaining a process, make sure you tell the whole story.
- **Too much information.** Be succinct.
- **Arbitrary classification or division.** Make sure your readers follow your logic and agree with your organization when you classify and divide objects and ideas.

- **Comparing apples and oranges.** When you discuss similarities and differences, make sure there's a clear point for the discussion that your readers can follow.

- **Missing causes or effects.** If you're writing a cause and effect story, make sure you clearly state both the cause and the effect. With this pattern, there's no need for subtlety.

- **Preaching to the choir.** The topic for arguments needs to be controversial. If you try to argue an insignificant point or an issue that your readers already agree with, there's no point. Your readers may feel you are patronizing them when you tell them something they already know. They can also think that your content is not credible.

- **Faulty logic.** Your readers will easily find holes in your logic; for example, the assumption that because event B follows event A, event A was the cause. Another classic argument that is often proven false is that if A equals B and B equals C, then A equals C.

> *The good writer seems to be writing about himself, but has his eye always on that thread of the Universe which runs through himself and all things.*
>
> —Ralph Waldo Emerson

Images and Rhetoric

An image can have a powerfully persuasive effect on your readers, evoking strong feelings, especially when it represents a controversial or charged topic, such as helmet laws (**FIGURE 10.1**), the tobacco industry, substance abuse, child labor, world hunger, obesity, overconsumption, and corporate greed.

FIGURE 10.1
California law mandates helmets for bikers, but not all states do.

A biker who felt the helmet law was an imposition might appeal to readers' pathos with an image showing how helmets restrict a biker's sense of freedom and joy.

You can find many examples of images on the Web that appeal to your emotions. To see several for antismoking campaigns, view www.thedesigninspiration.com/articles/top-45-creative-anti-smoking-advertisements.

Challenges

The best way to get better at writing Web content is to write, write some more, and rewrite. The challenges in this chapter focus on rhetorical modes.

Freewriting

The freewriting challenges in this chapter ask you to practice writing with rhetoric in mind.

Freewriting works best when it is timed. If you tend to write quickly, set the timer for ten minutes. If you tend to take a little more time, give yourself 15 minutes. Remember that with freewriting you don't need to worry about accuracy, grammar, spelling, and so forth.

LATE

Think about a time when you were late to an important event. Then tell either why you were late or explain the consequences of your tardiness.

COMPARE SONGS

Choose two songs that you enjoy. Describe the differences and similarities between the two songs.

Suggested Exercise

Exercises are longer projects that will take more time to complete. You can find more complete instructions, learning outcomes, and criteria for critiquing your work at www.write4web.com.

AN IMPORTANT LESSON

Write about a problem you caused or encountered and what the effects were.

Up Next

Now that you've reviewed rhetorical modes and considered strategies for structuring your Web content, you can move on to the next writing topic. Chapter 11, "Writing Instructions," describes how to write procedures that are clear and easy to follow.

11

Writing Instructions

You can find instructions on the Web for just about anything. Search and you will find. Do you need to entertain a few 11-year-olds for an afternoon? Google "mad science projects" to learn how to create volcanic crazy foam, green slime, and giant smoking bubbles. You'll find instructions for hundreds of wacky science adventures. Do you want to know how to prepare borscht soup or treacle tarts? Do you want insider tips on how to apply grip tape to your skateboard? Do you want to know how to drape a sari or tie a scarf? Have you been invited to a wedding reception, but you can't remember how to dance?

There are good reasons why you can find so many instructions. Your readers are hungry to understand how things work, learn new skills, and enjoy creative escapades with friends and family. Also, printed instructions that come in the box with purchased items are frequently lame, so readers turn to the Web where they expect to find better, more up-to-date information.

This chapter covers guidelines for writing effective, easy to follow, and fun step-by-step instructions, including how to:

- Meet your audience's needs
- Introduce the lesson
- Organize the content
- Test procedures

Know Your Audience

If you've read the previous chapters in this book, you know that your audience is a recurrent theme. To write instructions that are clear and meaningful for your readers, you must understand who they are. Have you gotten to know your audience, as suggested in Chapter 1, "All You Really Need to Know"? Did you develop a persona that describes the demographics for your archetypical reader? If your readers are 11, you'll adapt your tone and find words that are exciting for that age. If your readers have studied in Paris at Le Cordon Bleu, you won't explain how to cut butter into flour. If your readers don't have much discretionary income, you'll suggest they purchase after-market or secondhand goods from junkyards and thrift shops rather than expensive items from a high-end store. If your readers are under 30, the examples you use to illustrate your instructions should match the desires and needs of a young audience.

The more you know about your readers' demographics, the better you will be able to target your instructions to fit their needs.

Write for a Capable Reader

There's nothing worse than feeling that an author or a teacher is talking to you like you are six years old. Make sure your tone does not feel patronizing, and try not to dumb down your topics. If you consider yourself a guide or coach rather than a professor, you'll have an easier time adopting a casual, friendly tone.

What has annoyed you most about instructions that you've encountered? Missing steps? Too much information? Make a list of qualities you don't like to see in instructions.

This brief story helps to bring home the point: A road-sign committee was tasked to decide on the signage drivers would see upon entering and exiting a tunnel. The committee wanted drivers to turn their lights on for safety while driving through the tunnel. That part was easy. They decided the sign at the entrance would read *turn your lights on*. But a huge debate ensued about what drivers would read on the sign at the tunnel's exit. One person said it should say, *turn your lights off*. Another asked, but what if it is nighttime? So, another suggested, *turn your lights off unless it's nighttime*. Another committee member asked, "But what if the driver neglected to turn on his lights in the first place?" This discussion went on for some time until one wise committee member interjected, "Let's assume that the driver is not stupid." Finally, the committee arrived at an exit sign that would read *Lights On?* These two words were sufficient to remind drivers that they had turned their lights on. Most drivers are smart enough to decide whether or not they need their car lights on.

Don't Teach or Preach

Motion-studies photographer Harold "Doc" Edgerton captured images of stopped motion to show moments such as a speeding bullet bursting through an apple or the coronet shape a drop of milk made the instant it splashed onto a hard surface (http://edgerton-digital-collections.org). Edgerton, also a professor of electrical engineering at MIT, taught with methods and a philosophy that won over his students. "The trick to education," he said, "is to teach people in such a way that they don't realize they're learning until it's too late."

Instructional designers and teachers distinguish between two approaches in style. In one style, the teacher is the professor, the one who has all the answers—the "sage on the stage." A better approach is when the teacher is a guide or a coach. Your readers will feel more comfortable with your tone if you assume the role of guide rather than sage. There's no need to be self-deprecating. Your readers will appreciate a tone of confidence, not arrogance.

> *Nothing is impossible to a willing mind.*
>
> —Chinese proverb

Write for a Specific Skill Level

Recognize that individual readers have different levels of ability and skill. For almost any process or skill, some readers will be total beginners, some will have an intermediate skill level, and others will be more advanced.

If you want to write for varying levels of expertise, write separate instructions for each level, and then link them together.

Use Familiar Terms

Use the terms that your readers are most comfortable hearing. For example, if you're teaching your little sister how to ride a bike and she takes a spill, you'd describe her wounds as cuts, scrapes, or bruises. However, a doctor or a nurse might call those same wounds abrasions, hematomas, or contusions.

If your readers are skateboarders, you should know and use the accepted names of skateboarding tricks and not make up your own names and descriptions. You'll risk losing your readers' trust if you call a 360 a whirligig.

Don't Explain the Known

You don't need to explain common, everyday experiences that your reader already knows. For example, if you want readers to open a file, you don't need to go into great detail. Just say, *open the file*. If readers need to start an engine, don't try to explain that the key must go into the ignition, the car needs to be in neutral gear, and so on. Just say, *start the engine*.

Consider Multiple Learning Styles

It wasn't until the early '80s that American teachers became aware that there were multiple types of intelligence and began using more variety in their teaching techniques to meet the needs of students with multiple learning styles. (See the sidebar "Types of Intelligence.")

TYPES OF INTELLIGENCE

Do you learn best with images, with words, or with numbers? With multimedia, you can tailor your studies to favor your best learning styles. Howard Gardner first introduced the concept of multiple intelligences in 1983, pointing out that standard testing for IQ was far too limited. He identified seven types of intelligence:

1. **Linguistic intelligence.** With this type, you learn best by writing and reading.

2. **Logical-mathematical intelligence.** With this type, you learn best with patterns, categories, and relationships.

3. **Spatial intelligence.** With this type, you learn best with pictures.

4. **Bodily-kinesthetic intelligence.** With this type, you learn by doing through sensations.

5. **Musical intelligence.** With this type, you learn best by listening to sounds.

6. **Interpersonal intelligence.** With this type, you learn best by communication with others.

7. **Intrapersonal intelligence.** With this type, you learn by feelings.

To learn more about Howard Gardner's theory of multiple intelligences, see "The Seven Types of Intelligence" by Professor Lamp at www.professorlamp.com/ed/TAG/7_Intelligences.html.

---

try this

Do you know what your learning style is? The VARK (Visual, Aural, Read/Write, and Kinesthetic) questionnaire was developed to help individuals discover more about their learning style. You can try it out at www.vark-learn.com.

That's why multimedia works! You too can ensure that your instructions meet the needs of multiple learning styles by presenting your content with multiple media, such as text, voice-over, pictures, animation, and music.

If you remember all the fun and exciting ways you've learned on the Web, you'll want to make your best effort with your own contributions.

Just begin, and you'll be amazed at what you can accomplish.

Begin with an Introduction

Even if you're instructing readers on the simplest of procedures, make sure you introduce your topic. For example, if your instructions are for an easy recipe on how to make a grilled cheese sandwich, don't just jump into the steps or the ingredients; instead, warm up your readers with an overview, a summary, or an anecdote.

Depending on the topic and level of difficulty, you might include in your introduction some or all of the elements described in the next few sections.

It is better to light one candle than to curse the darkness.

—Chinese proverb

Start with an Anecdote

A great way to draw in your readers is to tell a story that relates to the topic of instruction. You might tell about your own introduction to the topic, or a lesson learned from your grandmother, or a childhood memory. For example, let's say you are providing a recipe for wild blueberry pie, and it's the same recipe your mother prepared every summer when your family vacationed in Northern Michigan. You might start with a story about how you helped your mom gather the blueberries but couldn't resist eating more than you collected. Maybe you were teased because your hands and lips were stained purple. You might tell how you'd wander into your mother's kitchen that was redolent with the smell of a hot, buttery crust and sugared berries while the pie baked.

Begin with the Big Picture

Your readers will have an easier time following instructions if you show them an image of the completed project. For example, if your instructions tell readers how to make a traditional Japanese paper crane, show the finished crane at the beginning of the story (**FIGURE 11.1**).

Think about a favorite snack or sweet that you enjoyed as a child. If you were to write instructions about preparing the food, how might you introduce it? Is there a funny or endearing story you can tell? Take a few notes on how you might develop an anecdote about this food.

FIGURE 11.1
Show the finished project in your introduction.

Describe Audience, Purpose, and Scope

Let your readers know at the beginning of the story who the instructions are intended for, what the purpose is, and what the scope is. Your readers' expectations will then be set appropriately.

For example, let's say your Photoshop lesson is aimed at showing beginners how to use the basic tools. For brevity, you might use the subtitles Audience, Purpose, and Scope to inform readers about the level of instruction. Then, if more advanced readers want tips for the expert user, such as how to mask an object in a photo and change its surface to reflective chrome, they'll understand immediately that they won't find this information in your beginner's lesson.

List Prerequisites

Tell readers up front about any skills or materials they'll need to complete the project or lesson. Here are the types of prerequisites you might include:

- Prior knowledge and where readers might obtain that knowledge
- Skills required
- Materials required
- Tools required
- Optional resources, such as background literature, helpful materials, and additional tools

If the list of prerequisites is somewhat complex, it's often helpful to provide a printable worksheet so readers can check off items as they obtain them.

List Benefits

Tell readers what they can expect to gain from the instructions. Make sure you state this as a benefit to your readers rather than what you think is cool or important about the topic. User guides in the '90s used to proclaim all the wonderful aspects of the product or service without acknowledging that the reader might not care if, say, the device offered 5 gigabytes of memory. Now many companies have become savvier. Rather than tell the story from the company's point of view, authors of these guides tell the story from the reader's perspective. The reader only cares about 5 gigabytes of memory if it translates to a faster, more efficient process.

What we have to learn to do, we learn by doing.

—Aristotle

Write Straightforward Steps

With instructions, it's best to be as brief as possible while still offering enough details so the reader can successfully master the task at hand.

Don't Explain Too Much

You don't need to go into great detail to explain steps to your reader. For example, if your instructions show readers how to use a software application, don't name every little part of the user interface and explain where everything is located. The majority of your readers will have a 15-inch screen, and there isn't really that much room on the screen for readers to get hopelessly lost. Trust that your readers will find common interface elements.

The following example shows too much detail and then a better step for exporting a file in a software application.

UNNECESSARY DETAIL	BETTER
Locate the File menu in the toolbar at the upper-left corner of the application. Click the menu, move the mouse down to the Export option, and click the mouse.	Choose File > Export.

Don't Explain Too Little

Nothing will frustrate your readers more than missing steps and incomplete information. Make sure you tell the whole story.

Keep Instructions Task Oriented

There's a temptation to write the bible of all bibles about a product or topic, especially if you love the product or if you've spent thousands of hours learning about a topic. You want to share everything you know, no matter how inconsequential. Companies that have spent lots of energy, time, and money on their products sometimes want to cover every small detail in their user guides. This temptation does not serve your readers well. Remember that Web readers are busy people. They'd much rather learn how to perform specific tasks than read encyclopedic details.

If you are writing instructions for the workplace, make sure you have a good understanding of how your readers perform typical tasks before you start writing any steps. That way your instructions will follow a scenario that your readers find familiar. If you introduce new and unfamiliar work flows, you're likely to lose the reader.

Use Clear, Consistent Titles and Subtitles

Your titles should let readers know what the instructions are about. Don't spend energy on creative wordplay, alliteration, irony, double meanings, or subtleties. Simply tell what readers will learn from the story.

The following examples illustrate clear, straightforward titles.

CLEAR TITLES		
How to Photograph Pets	Baking Cookies with Children	How to Juggle Three Balls

As you would with all Web content, break up the story into short modules of instruction. Use subtitles so the reader can quickly know what each module is about and move quickly through the steps. Remember to use a consistent format for titles and subtitles, as discussed in Chapter 2, "Best Practices for Writing for the Web."

Use Commands

Instructions are easiest to follow when you write them as commands. Think of what you would tell your dog Fido: Sit! Speak! Down! Start every sentence with a verb, like you are giving Fido a command. This is called *imperative mode*, and although you might feel a bit bossy, your readers will be comfortable with this mode. With instructions, your readers want to be told exactly what to do and how.

The following sentences illustrate instructions written in imperative mode.

EXAMPLE COMMANDS		
Place pattern pieces on the bias.	Insert the tab into slot B.	Apply the frosting as soon as the cake has cooled.

Use Active Voice

With active voice, there is a clear subject that takes on the action of the verb. By using active voice, your statements are clearer because the reader knows exactly who is performing the action. Active voice also allows you to use fewer words and keep the meaning of the sentence from getting too complicated.

The following sentence illustrates active voice. Remember that with imperative mode, the subject "you" is assumed.

ACTIVE VOICE	PASSIVE VOICE
Insert the tab into slot B.	The tab is inserted into slot B.

List Items with Numbers or Bullets

Remember that your readers can more easily and quickly grasp items when they are formatted as a list rather than described in paragraphs.

Number items that require a sequential order.

The following example illustrates partial instructions for making espresso. Notice that because the steps need to be in order, they are numbered.

TO MAKE ESPRESSO		
1. Fill the coffee machine's reservoir with cold water.	2. Lightly pack ground coffee in the coffee basket.	3. Slide the coffee basket in place.

Use bullets for items that have no particular order.

The following example offers suggestions for how to get rid of hiccups. Notice that because the items are not sequential, they are bulleted.

TO GET RID OF HICCUPS		
• Breathe into a paper bag.	• Drink a tablespoon of lemon juice.	• Think of a scary movie.

Break Up Lengthy Steps

Make sure you pace the instructions and don't continue on and on with steps. Readers will begin to tire after step nine. If your instructions have more than 12 steps, look for good places to break them up into separate modules. (For an example of poor instructions with far too many steps, see "Origami: The Crane," later in this chapter.)

Don't Nest Steps within Steps

Some instructions have a reasonable number of steps, but then there are steps within the steps that become tiresome. If you've read instructions that begin with numbered steps, and then one of the numbered steps has a subset of steps labeled a, b, c, and so on, you have experienced nested steps. Some authors go so far as to nest steps within nested steps and start labeling those steps with Roman numerals, which are difficult to follow. It's best to break the steps into separate modules and to keep the organization of each module broad rather than deep.

Keep Instructions Straightforward

Have you ever received directions from someone who gave you way too much information? You just wanted to know which street to watch for, yet you were told about a huge yellow building on the left where you could buy secondhand guitars, and sometimes a lady sells flowers on the corner where you should turn left, but she's not always there, in which case another vendor might be selling coffee, and on and on. You probably stopped listening at some point and made a note to yourself to get more straightforward directions from the Internet.

When writing the steps for instructions, don't mix in trivial or supplementary information. It's best to move quickly through the instructions, providing tasks in chronological order. When readers have to wade through too much information, it's easy for them to lose sight of the big picture and not follow the tasks at hand.

Link to Additional Information

If you feel your readers will benefit from additional information, add links to supplemental content. This gives readers a choice. If they want more information, they can follow the links. You might want to add links for the following types of information:

- Glossary definitions
- Tips
- Anecdotes
- Supplementary examples
- Additional resources

Provide Illustrations

For many projects, it's much easier for your reader to follow along if you provide illustrations or photos in addition to the written instructions.

If you've ever tried to read origami instructions without pictures, you know how difficult it is to follow someone's train of thought using only language.

The following example illustrates the impossibility of following instructions to fold the traditional origami crane without multiple pictures to guide you along the way (FIGURE 11.2).

Origami: The Crane

Posted on <u>August 20, 2011</u> by <u>Chelsea</u>

In Japan, the paper crane is a symbol of peace and luck. It's said that anyone who folds a thousand cranes will be granted a wish.

All you'll need is an 8-inch square sheet of origami paper.

To Fold the Crane

1. With the paper right side up (color showing) fold the square in half, diagonally, from corner to corner. It should now be a triangle.

2. Unfold it.

3. Repeat step 1 on the other side.

4. Unfold it.

5. Turn the paper over, so the white side is showing.

6. Fold the square in half.

7. Unfold it.

8. Repeat steps 6 and 7 on the other side.

9. Position the paper with one of the corners at the top.

10. This part is tricky. Using the creases you have made, bring the top three corners of the square down to the bottom corner. Flatten the creases, smashing the inside edges to the middle. It should now look like a folded square.

11. Fold the two flaps on either side of the square to the center. It should now look like a kite.

12. Unfold the flaps.

13. Fold top of model downwards and crease it well.

14. Unfold the flap.

15. Open the top flap and pull it up while pressing the two side flaps inwards.

16. Flatten everything down well.

17. Repeat steps 11 through 16 on the other side.

18. Next, fold the top flaps into the center.

19. Repeat on the other side.

20. Fold both bottom edges up to crease, and unfold.

21. Make an inside, reverse fold for each of the two edges you just creased.

22. On one side, make another inside reverse fold to form the head of the crane.

23. Fold down the side flaps to form the wings.

24. You're done!

FIGURE 11.2
Without illustrations, many instructions are too difficult to follow.

When you do show an image, make sure readers can see the object's orientation. If the image shows an object such as folded paper, ribbon, or cloth, readers need to be able to distinguish which side is up. Good illustrations use shading, cross-hatching, or lines to show, for example, the finished side of ribbon.

Show Motion with Video or Animation

Not surprisingly, video and animation provide the best way to instruct readers for movements, such as dance steps, juggling, exercises, and using tools to solder, hammer, and so forth.

Remember that video and animation production takes careful planning. You'll want to have a clear vision of your finished instructions before you start production. You'll need to know exactly what the viewer will see and hear. How will you introduce the topic? What motion graphics, voice-over, or other audio will you include? Chapter 4, "Adding Motion," and Chapter 5, "Adding Sound," offer suggestions for storyboarding and scripting as well as more guidelines for producing video, animation, and sound.

There are many benefits for adding instructional videos, including:

- **Increased viewer involvement.** Movies draw in your readers and hold their attention with a much stronger pull than any other media. Keep in mind that you're competing with other Web content and many other possible interruptions.
- **Change of pace.** Adding short video segments to written instructions gives readers a welcome break and adds interest to the story.
- **Audience learns more in less time.** It's much faster, easier, and more fun to have someone show you how to complete a project rather than to follow written instructions.
- **Speeding through boring moments.** When the process covers long periods of waiting, such as bread baking in the oven or paint drying, you can simply pause a second and then cut to the next interesting step. Your readers will be familiar with this transition and will happily jump forward in time.
- **Added personalization.** Instructions can seem cold and dry, especially when they explain a software application or an extremely technical process. You can always add interest and energy with an enthusiastic speaker.
- **Added versatility and diversity.** Using different speakers, you can quickly show alternate perspectives, cultural differences, and various approaches to solving problems.
- **Added viewer interaction and control.** The playback viewers offer readers flexibility and the ability to tailor their viewing experience with controls to fast forward, pause, or replay.

End on a Positive Note

When you've finished the last step in your instructions, end with a brief impression or anecdote to give the story a sense of completion. For recipes, you might just say how irresistible the meal will be. (If you watch cooking shows, the cook always takes a bite of the prepared dish at the end of the show and says, "mmmmm.")

You might think you are done at this point, but you have one last, important task. When the instructions are complete, you need to test them.

Test, Test, Test

The reason some cookbooks, such as Julia Child's *Mastering the Art of French Cooking*, are so successful is that the recipes have been thoroughly tested by numerous cooks in several environments.

To test your instructions:

1. Set up an environment similar to what your readers will have while following your instructions.
2. Find a volunteer who is representative of your readers to follow your written instructions.
3. Provide the volunteer with the instructions.
4. Don't talk during the testing. This is important. If you begin to explain the written instructions, the test is not valid. Simply watch and take notes.
5. Ask questions, only when the test is done, if you need clarification on what the volunteer understood or if there were problems with specific steps in the instruction.
6. Revise the instructions according to your findings during the test.
7. Repeat testing the instructions until you are happy with the results.

Challenges

The best way to get better at writing Web content is to write, write some more, and rewrite. The challenges in this chapter focus on procedures.

Freewriting

The freewriting challenge in this chapter asks you to practice writing with procedures in mind.

Freewriting works best when it is timed. If you tend to write quickly, set the timer for ten minutes. If you tend to take a little more time, give yourself

15 minutes. Remember that with freewriting you don't need to worry about accuracy, grammar, spelling, and so forth.

SOMETHING I LEARNED AS A CHILD

Write about a process you were taught when you were a kid. Did you knit a scarf or make paper chains with gum wrappers? Did you assemble model cars or planes? Did you learn to fish? Did you tumble rocks? Write for a reader who is the same age that you were when you learned the process.

Suggested Exercise

Exercises are longer projects that will take more time to complete. You can find more complete instructions, learning outcomes, and criteria for critiquing your work at www.write4web.com.

PAPER PROJECT

Write instructions for folding an airplane or any other paper project, such as making a hat, a gift box, or an envelope. Consider using construction paper, newsprint, grocery bags, wallpaper samples, or other paper materials. List any materials required in your introduction. Make sure you include illustrations.

Up Next

You now have all the information you need to provide clear and easy-to-read instructions to your readers. With another piece of the writing for the Web puzzle completed, you're ready to move on to something completely different yet just as important. Chapter 12, "Writing Blogs," offers suggestions for choosing your topics and writing a succession of blogs that will keep your readers coming back for more.

12

Writing Blogs

Are you already blogging? Maybe you'd like to start blogging, but you're not sure what to blog about? The blogosphere has grown up over the last decade; blogs today cover an incredibly diverse range of topics.

If you're eager to experiment, you'll want to read this chapter for ideas about:

- Choosing a theme
- Writing a succession of stories
- Staying motivated and inspired
- Managing reader comments

What Exactly Is a Blog?

The term *blog* blends the words *web* and *log*. If you think that blogs are personal stories, such as diaries, travel journals, and accounts of family gatherings, you're right. If you think that blogs cover stories about politics, activism, economics, entertainment, and health and fitness, you're also right. The tools to blog have become so easy to use that these days anyone can blog, whether you're young, old, nontechnical, tech-savvy, rich, or poor. The blogosphere is a democracy. Anyone and everyone can have a voice on the Web.

Wait until you are hungry to say something, until there is an aching in you to speak.

—Natalie Goldberg

The term blog is used in two ways: for a blog site, where the collection of individual blog posts reside, and for each post on the blog site.

Some people distinguish between various types of blogging and microblogging (a tweet is a microblog). However, Jon Sobel, author of "State of the Blogosphere, 2010," says that "the lines between blogs, micro-blogs, and social networks are disappearing" (http://technorati.com/blogging/article/state-of-the-blogosphere-2010-introduction).

Getting Started with Blogging

Posting blogs on any topic that you choose only takes time, planning, and access to the Internet. If you're not ready to take on your own series of blog posts on your own blog site, you can just dip your toes into the blogosphere by writing a story and submitting it to the editors of a blog site that's already established. Or, you can jump wholeheartedly into the deep end and start your own blog site.

To get started with any blog, you'll first want to gather ideas for topics to write about.

Finding Inspiration for Blog Topics

An inspirational notebook, whether it's digital or paper, is a great tool to help you gather ideas for writing blogs. Start by thinking about and listing your passions. What gets you all fired up? What makes you mad? What makes you smile? How do you spend your weekends? Take the time to reflect on all the things that you find inspirational. Do you like old movies? Is it fun to go to museums? Is fashion your passion? Are you planning your next hike in the backcountry? Jot down anything that floats your boat in your notebook.

Choosing Topics and Themes

Common advice is to write about what you know. Although this is good advice, remember too that you'll be spending a great deal of time on any topic you choose. To make sure you don't get bored, choose a topic that you want to know more about.

The following suggestions are starting points for your own lists.

INSPIRATIONAL PLACES	
Hideaways in the city, suburbs, or country	
Places you've travelled, amusement parks, art galleries, botanical gardens, concert halls	
YOUR FAMILY	
Your ancestors	Someone who has influenced you
A relative who is a character	What it's like being a parent, a sibling, or an only child
Awkward family moments	How you celebrate the holidays
Family pets	Family traditions
YOU	
What makes you laugh?	What are your hopes and dreams?
What causes are you passionate about?	What are your hobbies?
What is it like to live in the country of your birth?	What sports do you participate in or watch?
What bothers you?	What would you do if you won a million dollars?
What games do you like?	Are you a collector?

YOUR FAVORITES			
Books	Musicians	Artists	Comedians
Movies	Drinks	Restaurants	Recipes

Examine Your Life

try this

Draw a picture of your childhood bedroom. Make the drawing as detailed as you can. Use the picture as a catalyst for lists in your notebook.

Socrates said that "the unexamined life is not worth living." If you examine your life, you'll find you have plenty to blog about.

A great starting point is your childhood. Where did you live when you were five years old? Where did you go to grade school? What was your home like? A treasure trove of ideas can come from memories of your childhood bedroom. What were your parents like? Were you allowed to decorate your own room? Would your mom have allowed you to spray paint the walls? Did you share the room with a sibling? What toys did you play with? What was the neighborhood like? What games did you play with other kids on the block?

Write the Blog You Want to Read

try this

Draw a picture of your childhood neighborhood. Make sure you draw the street you lived on and all the places where you explored and played near your house. Use the picture as a catalyst for lists in your notebook.

Toni Morrison said, "If there is a book that you want to read, but it hasn't been written yet, you must be the one to write it." The same truth applies to blogs. If there's a blog you want to read, but you haven't found it yet, you must write it.

Of course, you'll want to choose a topic that someone else wants to read as well. After all, why would you bother to post a blog for all the world to see if it's only for your own enjoyment?

Let's say, for example, that you love all things about French culture. You've been to France several times, and you know you want your blog to appeal to other Francophiles. First, look online to see what blogs are similar to the one you want to write but have qualities you don't find appealing. Second, evaluate what you like and don't like, and decide how yours will be a hundred times better. Maybe some of the blogs don't feel sincere or don't seem exciting enough given the topic. Third, once you've decided to begin your own blog and have determined the topic is France, you then need to find the niche or angle that you'll take on this topic.

Narrow or Broaden Your Topic

When you've settled on a theme that you'd like to blog about, you can then decide whether your topic is too broad, too narrow, or just right for the direction you want the blog to take.

For example, a blog about France as a general topic is much too broad. To narrow the topic, focus on a more specific aspect you enjoy about France. Maybe you like chatting with expats in France, or you're crazy about the painters who started impressionism. Make a list of everything you like about the broader topic and think through each item on your list. When you come up with a more specific topic, your audience will also be more defined.

If you've decided on a very narrow topic for your blog, and you're afraid you won't have enough of an audience or enough to write about, you can always broaden the topic. For example, let's say that you are fascinated with Japanese crafts and particularly love a pattern that you use to knit Japanese flip-flops. A blog on Japanese flip-flops seems too narrow, so to broaden it, you might try listing all the reasons you love the activity and the patterns you use to knit them. Depending on your interests, you might broaden this topic to ethnic knitting or Japanese crafts, or some more general aspect of flip-flops.

> *Anybody who has survived his childhood has enough information about life to last him the rest of his days.*
>
> —Flannery O'Connor

Composing a Succession of Stories

Every artist would like to have a body of work that reflects the artist's abilities and sensibilities. Besides skill and talent, the qualities an artist needs for the long range are stamina, patience, tenacity, curiosity, and courage. As a blogger, the body of work you produce requires these same ingredients.

You'll need to develop strategies to continually discover and write about new material. You'll also need strategies to stay motivated and inspired.

Staying Motivated and Inspired

If you're like most writers, there will be times when your enthusiasm lags or you just don't feel moved or energized. Some call this bloggers' block. What can you do?

Here are a few things to try to placate your muse:

- **Move.** Any movement, but especially repetitive motion sports, such as jogging, swimming, walking, or bicycling, not only stimulates endorphins, but also puts you in the right frame of mind for telling stories.
- **Listen to music.** Music boosts your brain power, lifts your spirits, and invigorates your body. Listening to an old song can stir up memories of events in your life when you heard the same song.
- **Light a scented candle.** Fragrances have a powerful effect on mood and memory. Your sense of smell is the only sense that the brain experiences directly.
- **Eat chocolate.** If you like chocolate, the smell, the taste, the texture, the sweetness, the caffeine, and the pleasant sensation as anxiety subsides and your moods elevate will pull you back into writing mode.

For more ideas, see the sidebar "Inside the Coffin."

INSIDE THE COFFIN

Diane Ackerman describes quirky methods famous writers have developed to woo their muse in "O Muse! You Do Make Things Difficult" (www.nytimes.com/1989/11/12/books/o-muse-you-do-make-things-difficult.html). In the article for the *New York Times*, she begins, "Dame Edith Sitwell used to lie in an open coffin for a while before she began her day's writing. When I mentioned this macabre bit of gossip to a poet friend, he said acidly, 'If only someone had thought to shut it.'"

Here are a few examples of the rituals:

- Ernest Hemingway wrote standing up.

- Benjamin Franklin wrote while taking a bath. (Ackerman also likes to write in the bathtub.)

- Mark Twain wrote lying down.

- Gertrude Stein wrote poetry in her Ford, parked in front of her house.

- Stephen King takes a vitamin and then writes.

- Charles Dickens liked to walk 20–30 miles before writing.

- The poet Schiller inhaled the smell from rotten apples he kept in his writing desk.

try this

Think about a ritual you'd like to test or one that you've already developed. You might light a candle, play soft music, or chew gum. Some authors doodle or write letters as a warm-up exercise.

Making the Commitment

Good writing takes time and effort. You've probably heard Thomas Edison's wise words: "Genius is one percent inspiration, ninety-nine percent perspiration." It's good to listen for your muse, but if it's not available, you still need to make the effort without it.

A professional writer is an amateur who didn't quit.

—Richard Bach

Set goals for your writing practice and stick to them. You can establish goals by time, word count, page count, or blog count. Some writers use a timer or some other method to track the time they spend daily on their writing. See the sidebar "The Egg Timer Method."

Every writer struggles with finding quality time for writing. Some of the best authors squeeze their daily practice in while parenting, managing households, and working day jobs.

THE EGG TIMER METHOD

Author Chuck Palahniuk, in "13 Writing Tips" (http://chuckpalahniuk.net/workshop/essays/chuck-palahniuk), offers this first tip: "When you don't want to write, set an egg timer for one hour (or half hour) and sit down to write until the timer rings."

After the timer goes off, chances are that you'll still feel like writing and continue for another hour or so. Some writers who use this method don't have the luxury of taking the entire hour in one go. They start the timer, write for 20 minutes or so, and then turn off the timer. Later in the day, they start the timer again and write for another segment of time, stopping and starting the timer each time they sit down to write until they have met their goal of one hour for the day.

Challenge Yourself

Some writers like to give themselves challenges, which are a little like New Year's resolutions, but you're more likely to adhere to a challenge. Here are a few examples:

- **365, or a daily post.** This challenge is especially popular with photo bloggers. The idea is that you will post daily. For photographers, that means at the end of one year, you'll have posted 365 photos. The difficulty with this challenge is that it's not easy to get an excellent shot every day. You can find several 365-photo challenges on Flickr and Tumblr.
- **52, or a weekly post.** This challenge gives you more time to post quality content and is a bit more reasonable than trying to post a blog a day.
- **5-day challenge.** Challenge yourself to post new blogs for five days straight.
- **Blog Month.** National Novel Writing Month occurs during November of every year. Participants challenge themselves to write a novel in a month (175 pages or 50,000 words). Give yourself a similar challenge to write 40,000 words in the month of your choice.

Create your own challenge that suits your style and available time. Make sure you're up for any challenge you accept, and stay honest with yourself about whether or not the quality of your posts is suffering because you have steeled yourself to complete the challenge. You don't want to lose readership because you were afraid to let go of a challenge.

Give yourself a three-day challenge, writing a post a day for three days on related topics.

Organize a Blogging Critique Group

Meeting regularly with a critique group can help you improve your writing skills and obtain feedback on your blogs. Read Chapter 13, "Re-Vision," for more details about working with critique groups.

Sustaining Readership

Blogs are a great medium for building community, developing relationships, and cultivating loyal readers. In the best of circumstances, your readers will be excited about the stories on the blog site, will comment freely, and will develop the habit of returning to your site again and again.

How can you gain and keep your readers' respect and loyalty? Chapter 10, "A Refresher on the Rhetorical Modes," offers guidelines to ensure that your readers find you a credible author. You'll find a few more suggestions in the next section.

Writing Credible Blogs

Ask a buddy to spend about an hour with you and explain that you will each write a draft of the other's bio. Decide what type of information you want in your bio, and let your buddy know. You will each spend about 15 minutes interviewing the other. After asking several questions, each of you should write a first draft of a bio. Trade your work with your buddy. Then rewrite the draft, composing a bio that you can post on your blog site.

If your readers suspect that you have ulterior motives or don't have scruples, they will not want to be a part of your blog. To keep your readers' trust, make sure you:

- Maintain high standards for your blog posts.
- Make every effort to avoid errors. If there is an error, correct it quickly.
- Provide fair and impartial opinions and reviews.
- If you are paid to endorse products or receive gifts from the manufacturer, disclose this information to your readers.
- Give attribution to any ideas or Web content that is not your original concept.
- Don't stuff keywords into your content. If you write naturally for your audience, the content will automatically contain keywords. (If you're not familiar with keywords, they help search engines find your content.) Although it's important that your Web site and content are easily found, you don't have to sacrifice good sentence structure for the sake of inserting a keyword.

Include a Bio

Your readers will appreciate a picture of you and a short bio on the Web site so they have a sense of who you are and why you are writing the blog. Make sure the bio somehow relates to the main theme of your blogs. For example, if your blog is about skateboarding, include in your bio some information about how you became involved in the sport.

Include Information About the Site

Add information about your site so new readers can quickly understand the main focus of the blog.

Here are a few items you might include in the About section:

- A very brief, clear description of the blog site's main focus
- Who the main contributors are for the site
- The motivation for starting the site
- How long the site has been in existence

Include Guidelines for Reader Comments

Let your readers know that you welcome their comments, but also that you have a few guidelines they need to follow if they want you to post their comments. Make sure you moderate all comments to ensure a safe, fair environment on your site.

Encourage Reader Comments

Respond to reader comments quickly and frequently. Although Happy Talk is generally discouraged, when responding to readers, you'll want to be a little more chatty and sociable. If you use short, choppy sentences, the reader can interpret your responses as cold or negative. If the reader asks a question, don't just answer with one word, "No," or two words, "You cannot." Give a longer explanation. You might say something on the order of, "Thanks for your suggestion. We did try that tactic, and honestly, it didn't work out well because," and finish the sentence with the reason.

The Eskimos had fifty-two names for snow because it was important to them; there ought to be as many for love.

—Margaret Atwood

Here are a few more suggestions:

- Ignore rants and flames. If you try to respond to them, you'll get tangled up in someone else's emotional drama.
- Be gracious when someone corrects you.
- Keep an upbeat tone.
- Remember to praise and thank your readers for any ideas, creativity, enthusiasm, and encouragement.

Keep Content Fresh

Some bloggers republish older posts with a few new twists and a slightly different title. Your loyal readers have good memories, and you don't need to rehash old content if you have strategies for developing fresh content.

The main idea behind the following tactics is to mix it up by relying on multiple authors, media, genres, and storylines. The variety not only helps you to come up with more ways of posting, but keeps the delivery of your posts well paced and novel:

- **Collaborate with multiple authors.** Authors can contribute posts individually, or several authors can collaborate on single posts.
- **Ask guest authors to contribute.** Ask an expert on a topic related to your blog site's theme to write an article. You might also be a guest on another blog to get more exposure for your blog site.
- **Mix up the media.** Post photo blogs, vlogs (video blogs), podcasts, and animations.
- **Add posts with a variety of genres.** Add different types of posts, such as instructions, reviews and critiques, white papers, announcements, contests, and so forth.
- **Add feature stories.** If you've watched the *Rocky and Bullwinkle Show*, you know that each episode has regular features, such as *Bullwinkle's Corner*, *Mr. Know-It-All*, and *Dudley Do-Right of the Mounties*. Devise similar types of feature stories for your blog site with fresh content in repeated formats. For example, you might have a "Did you know?" blog that appears regularly with random, interesting facts related to your blog's theme. Another example might be a regular feature called "Mama's Kitchen" that features recipes and meals related to your blog's theme.
- **Follow your dreams.** Why not follow your wildest dreams and highest hopes with your blogging? If you're having fun composing the content, your audience will have fun reading it.

Pursue Your Passions

When you're having a blast researching and writing your blog, your readers will feel the excitement in your work. Writing for a responsive audience has a lot of rewards, but the best part is that you get to plan and execute all sorts of fun activities and adventures, and call it research for your blog.

Challenges

The best way to get better at writing Web content is to write, write some more, and rewrite. The challenges in this chapter focus on self-examination and writing blogs.

Freewriting

The freewriting challenge in this chapter asks you to practice writing with blogging in mind.

Freewriting works best when it is timed. If you tend to write quickly, set the timer for ten minutes. If you tend to take a little more time, give yourself 15 minutes. Remember that with freewriting you don't need to worry about accuracy, grammar, spelling, and so forth.

A ROOM OF ONE'S OWN

In her essay "A Room of One's Own," Virginia Woolf states, "... a woman must have money and a room of her own if she is to write fiction." You can read the full text online at http://gutenberg.net.au/ebooks02/0200791.txt.

Where is it that you work best? Write about your writing room or space. Describe what it looks like and smells like, and how you feel as you are writing in it. Is it messy or neat? Empty or full? Expansive or tiny? Do you have a formal desk? Do you write sitting up or lying down?

Suggested Exercise

Exercises are longer projects that will take more time to complete. You can find more complete instructions, learning outcomes, and criteria for critiquing your work at www.write4web.com.

POST A BLOG

Post a blog on a topic of your choice, or select one of the following suggestions for your topic:

- What will the World Wide Web look like in five years?
- Are blogs literature?
- If you were forced to write a blog a day on any topic, what would it be and why would you choose it?
- If you had to put only one bumper sticker on your car, what would it say?
- What sport or athletic activity do you enjoy? What are the main benefits of the sport?

Up Next

By now you probably have a good idea of what you want to write and some strategies to keep writing. The next chapter, "Re-Vision," asks you to take a second and third look at stories you've written. Some say that writing is rewriting.

13

Re-vision

All artists need to find points in time when they can detach, stand back, reenvision their work in progress, and evaluate it with a fresh perspective. Revising Web content is an art; the revision methods that work best for one author may or may not work best for you. This chapter encourages you to explore different approaches to reenvisioning and rewriting, and to discover more about what works best for you and your style of revision, including:

- How to take a new look at your work
- Accepting criticism with an open mind
- Working with a critique group
- Deciding when your story is finished

Writing Is Rewriting

All you have to do is write one true sentence. Write the truest sentence that you know.

—Ernest Hemingway

All writing is, in fact, rewriting. The moment the words emerge on paper, you have already unconsciously or consciously sifted through several other word choices and ways to say what you initially placed on the page. As your story unfolds and the words materialize on the page, your progress involves a dance among fleeting moments of writing, reviewing, and rewriting.

Many books about writing divide the writing process into stages that more or less include the following:

- **Planning.** This stage, often called prewriting, involves brainstorming and trial and error to decide on your main theme, the structure of the story, and most of the elements you will include. You might use any number of tools for the planning stage, such as mind maps, 3x5 cards, outlines, sticky notes, free-writing, and storyboards.

- **First draft.** This stage involves composing a draft that flows logically and has a beginning, middle, and end. The story is not yet polished, but it feels somewhat complete.

- **Revision.** During this stage, you look for problems with the story, editing and rewriting with an eye for holes in the logic, missing transitions, anecdotes and examples that are out of order, and so forth. If your first draft doesn't have an exciting hook or a satisfying end, you revise the beginning and ending as needed. Some misunderstand the art of revision and think that this process only involves fixing a few cosmetic errors. But for this stage, you need to look at the big picture: You need tools equivalent to a hammer, a saw, and an axe, and you need to use a lot of muscle.

- **Proofreading.** When you are done with major rewriting, you proofread, polishing the final draft by fixing grammatical errors, misspelled words, and typos. For proofreading, you need tools equivalent to fine-grit sandpaper and a polishing cloth.

Take a few minutes to think about your current writing process, which isn't necessarily the one described in this section. Does it help you achieve your writing goals? Would you like to make any changes?

Deciding When to Rewrite

It's wise to revise but only when rewriting improves the work and doesn't hamper your creativity and continued progress. While you're in the midst of writing a first draft, pounding away at the keyboard as your ideas and impressions materialize on the page, your main task is to pull together all your thoughts in one place. It's not the time to worry about misspelled words or smooth transitions.

During the early stages of writing, you don't want that inner, critical-editor voice sitting on your shoulder and scolding in your ear, "No, no, no. That sounds terrible. You idiot; dicombooberate isn't a real word!" Before you have a completed draft, it's also not the best time to ask others for feedback. All negativity at this point can delay the process, send you on wild goose chases, and make you anxious. It's not a good time to try to please a critic, especially when that reviewer won't have a true vision of the finished work. *You* might not even have that true vision yet.

On the other hand, while writing the first draft, you might get caught up in the fun and excitement of invention, and the pure joy of splashing around in a pool of words. This high energy can make you feel that the writing you've just finished is absolutely wonderful, and you couldn't possibly make it any better.

Because you are so close to your work as you're composing, it's difficult to see the big picture and notice where the story goes astray or gets cloudy and confusing. It's also tough to see the smaller errors, because they've become too familiar. For these reasons, when you've completed your first draft, you'll need to get some distance from it before you begin rewriting.

Re-vision Tactics

Once you have a draft in place, you're ready to roll up your sleeves and begin editing. But you first need to find a way to reexamine the work and evaluate it with new eyes. You already know the difficulty of evaluating your writing at this point because you've become too close to it. Fortunately, there are plenty of tactics you can take to get some distance.

PUT THE WORK ASIDE

Most authors can become more detached from a story they're working on by putting it aside for a designated period of time. See the sidebar "How Long Should I Set My Work Aside?"

There's a fine line between putting a work aside to get distance and taking more time than you need because you're procrastinating. Sometimes you don't have as much time as you'd like to get distance, because you have a deadline to meet.

The essence of cinema is editing. It's the combination of what can be extraordinary images of people during emotional moments, or images in a general sense, put together in a kind of alchemy.

—Francis Ford Coppola

Do you have any strategies for silencing the inner voice/editor when you don't want to listen? If not, can you think of any that might work? (You might imagine stuffing a sock in her mouth.)

HOW LONG SHOULD I SET MY WORK ASIDE?

When you've finished a draft and have put it aside to gain a fresh perspective, how long should you wait to have another look and begin revisions? The answer probably depends on the nature of the draft, the genre, the audience, and your available time to finish the work.

In North Country Public Radio's article "Art 'word of the month': revise," the author points out that Roman poet Horace thought it was appropriate to wait nine years before revising a work of art (www.northcountrypublicradio.org/news/story/11143/20080327/ art-word-of-the-month-revise). If that seems excessive, consider the story of Beethoven's work, which is included in the accompanying podcast. Composer Paul Siskind's audio narration states that it is known from Beethoven's notes that he continued revising the cello melody that opens the second movement of his Fifth Symphony over a period of eight years.

For a completely opposite point of view, in *From Where You Dream*, edited by Janet Burroway (Grove Press, 2005), author Robert Olen Butler says that for fiction, it's crucial that you write every day to stay in the same zone that a story demands. While writing his fifth novel, Butler had to take two months off to move to a new home. When he returned to his novel eight weeks later, he stated, "It took eight weeks of daily torture to write a single sentence—because I'd stopped writing every day."

List five or six activities you might use to take a mini break from writing. Either list activities that are so engaging that you can think of nothing else or so relaxing that you don't think.

The following scenarios can, in a short timeframe, make you feel as though you've taken a longer break:

- **Watch a good movie.** Movies pull you out of this world and into their own place in time. With a good movie, you'll lose yourself in the story and won't have a thought about your own writing until the movie ends.
- **Soak in a bubble bath.** Submerge yourself in water to displace all your sensibilities and forget all your worries.
- **Juggle.** Choose an activity that doesn't allow you to think about anything else. Ten minutes of juggling, jumping rope, or playing chess requires complete concentration.
- **Call a friend.** Talk about anything but your writing.
- **Take in a sunset.** Immerse yourself in nature's beauty (**FIGURE 13.1**). Watch the sun set; clouds float past a crescent moon; or deep, glassy waves break as they head toward the shore.

FIGURE 13.1
A beautiful sunset can
clear your mind.

CHANGE YOUR PERSPECTIVE

When you want your work to look fresh and new, you can trick your eyes by changing the view of a story. Here are a few suggestions:

- **Zoom in.** Use the Zoom In button to magnify any part of the story you want to focus on in more detail. The larger print will slow you down, and the larger font makes the story look new and different.

- **Zoom out.** Use the Zoom Out button to reduce your story until it just looks like greeking (it will be illegible). Use this view to look at the big picture. Are there any paragraphs that are too long or too short? Does the overall structure look OK?

- **Preview a private draft.** Most editors, including blog editors, allow you to choose several different views of a draft. You can also publish your blog as a private post. By choosing any of these options, you can see the work in different views prior to publishing and get a fresh perspective.

- **Make a PDF.** Make a PDF file of your draft, and view it with the Acrobat viewer, which allows you to choose multiple view options.

- **Print a hard copy.** Print the story on paper to get a better view.

- **Read the work from end to beginning.** Looking backwards at your work can reveal flaws in how it flows.

- **Tape yourself reading the story and play it back.** While you're taping, you'll notice where the story lags. As you play it back, listen for places where you stumble on words or don't sound enthusiastic. Pay attention to any spot where your mind wanders as you are reading.

- **Ask someone else to read your story out loud.** Notice which words are emphasized when someone else reads. Pay attention to how the story is interpreted. Also, note any words that get in the way; places where the story drags; or where the reader seems to lose interest, get confused, or sound mechanical. You can hear everything that is wrong and right in a story by listening to the voice.
- **Wear a funny hat or hold a red pencil in your hand while you're reading.** Don't laugh; this is a trick that can work. If it doesn't, have a good laugh.

BIG PICTURE RE-VISION

Before you begin rewriting, make sure you take a holistic approach, looking over the entire story as a unified piece before tackling individual paragraphs. Are there sections that don't belong and simply clutter the story line? For more information about removing clutter from your story, be sure to read Chapter 7, "Writing Succinctly." Do you need to layer in more information because the story is incomplete? Does the story have a clear beginning, middle, and end?

The power of imagination makes us infinite.

—John Muir

ASK FOR HELP

Find someone you trust who will treat your work with respect and can show you where you need improvement. If that person is your mother, know that she will most likely find more to praise than to criticize. That's fine, but you may want to seek others.

Ideally, you'll find more than one person to critique your writing. Working with an entire group of reviewers on a regular basis that can give your work the attention it deserves can help tremendously.

Workshops and Critiques

One of the best ways to get feedback on your work is to join or form a critique group. The benefits of regularly meeting with a steady group of like-minded writers include:

- **Meeting deadlines.** Having to show your work to the group at regular intervals imposes due dates. You'll find you get more done because you have a schedule, and you won't want to miss the opportunity to get your stories critiqued.
- **Sharing discoveries.** When you meet with others, you'll naturally share what works well and what doesn't work for writing for the Web. You and the other authors might plan time during meetings for more general discussions and socializing.

- **Networking.** Besides tips on writing and publishing on the Web, your critique group can also network, sharing information about Web sites with appealing content, contests, and practical advice about working habits, motivation, and so forth.

- **Developing a thicker skin.** It's hard for beginners to share work and take immediate, constructive feedback gracefully. The more you work with others, however, the better you are able to listen with an open mind and not become defensive.

- **Forming lasting friendships.** Very often, you'll find kindred spirits within the critique group.

Working with a Critique Group

If you join a critique group, make sure you benefit from group activities and don't waste precious writing time or get frustrated.

The critiques you receive from a group can help or hinder your writing process. Ideally, when your work gets reviewed, there will be a good mix of comments that do the following:

- **Encourage.** Comments that either encourage you to keep working on a particular story or encourage you as an author and your writing practice.

- **Praise.** Comments that point out what works well in your stories.

- **Suggest rewriting.** Comments that point out where the story needs rework. The criticism must focus on an individual story; comments that criticize the author are never helpful.

If the group is not yet established, be sure to discuss all your options and agree on a few rules. If the group is already established and you don't like the way it functions, either find another group or ask for changes.

For new groups, be sure to discuss:

- **Where you will meet.** Does the group meet online? If so, how do you share manuscripts? Do you use meeting software or social media? If the group meets face to face (F2F), where will you meet? Do you prefer a neutral place, such as a library or coffee shop? Or, would you rather meet in each other's homes?

- **When you will meet.** Most groups set up a regular time, such as the first Tuesday of every month, morning or evening, depending on group members' availability. If you're meeting online and there's no set time, who will be the scheduler? For online critiques, you need to have someone in charge to make sure everyone turns in their work on a certain date and everyone participates before a certain date.

- **Whether there will be snacks or drinks.** If you're meeting at someone's home, is anyone responsible for snacks or drinks? How will you manage refreshments so they don't interfere with critiques?
- **How you will manage the critique process.** If you're meeting F2F, will you bring copies of the work? Will you email them ahead of time? What will the lineup be to make sure everyone gets a fair chance for critiques? How much time will you allow for each member?

Here are a few recommendations for a successful critique group meeting:

- **Don't allow the author to speak during the critique.** Ask someone else to read the work out loud. Make sure everyone gets a chance to offer suggestions and feedback. If you are the author, simply sit and listen. Stay open minded and try not to get defensive, even if the critiques aren't favorable. When all suggestions have been offered, then you can talk. Ask questions if you aren't clear about anything that was said. Ask for clarity if someone only gave generalities. Don't accept vague feedback, such as "It didn't work for me." Ask for specifics. Even if the critique is "I really liked this," ask for specifics.
- **Make sure your critiques are fair, truthful, and constructive.** If you don't have anything nice to say, find something redeemable in the work. Give suggestions for re-envisioning as well as rewriting.
- **Show up on time.** Don't waste everyone's time and concentration by arriving late.
- **Keep the meeting on track.** If the discussion starts to wander off topic, gently bring the focus back to the critique. If group members need time to socialize and chat about life in general, suggest regular breaks.
- **Assign someone the task of chairing the meeting.** That person can establish who goes first, how much time you have for each work, when you take a break, and when the meeting is over. Rotate this responsibility so everyone feels a part of the meeting and no one feels overburdened.
- **Decide if other topics are agreeable to everyone.** If time allows, you might discuss good reads, exceptional blogs, writing workshops and classes, or other related activities.

Devise a Critique Worksheet

You can save time and keep the group focused by having a set of criteria that the group regularly uses to evaluate each work. If you decide on the criteria as a group, there will be much less resistance to following it.

Use the sample criteria for evaluation shown in **TABLE 13.1** as a starting point, but take the time as a group to develop a new worksheet that reflects the group's decisions on how to evaluate each other's work.

TABLE 13.1 Sample Evaluation Criteria for Critique Group

	EXCELLENT (A)	OK (B)	WEAK (C)
Demonstrates effective storytelling techniques.	Story begins with a hook, in media res. The story is developed with an inverted pyramid. It is focused and clear, holds the reader's interest, and advances the main idea. The final paragraph brings the story to a resolution or conclusion.	Story does not begin at an interesting point but has enough focus to maintain the reader's interest.	The main themes are not clear. The content is flat with no tension or development. It feels like the story could end at any point. There are no "gold coins" dropped along the way to keep the reader engaged.
Creates a voice, style, and tone appropriate for the audience.	Story reveals the author's unique voice. Tone fits the topic and the intended audience. Style engages readers and feels credible. The style and content are designed for a specific audience.	Author's style is either flat or the tone is inconsistent. The story is not engaging. Author seems tentative.	Author's style and tone are inconsistent. Tone is pedantic or doesn't sound authentic. It is not clear who the intended audience is.
Presents multimedia elements and linked pages effectively.	Media fits the story, flows with the text, tells part of the story, and has a professional presentation. Links are well thought out and easy to navigate.	Media is adequate for the story but does not flow well or add much.	Media is missing or does not fit the story. The story feels incomplete because the media is not taking on its fair share of the weight of the story.
Story develops with logical organization and effective structure.	Story has a strong sense of direction. Paragraphs support the main ideas and stay on topic.	Story and central themes are evident. Paragraphs are a mixture of generalizations and details that support the main direction of the story.	Story does not have enough substance or is not developed. Supporting paragraphs are too general and inconsistent with story's direction.

table continues on next page

TABLE 13.1 *continued*

	EXCELLENT (A)	OK (B)	WEAK (C)
Good sentence structure, precise wording, and effective language.	Word choice is precise and fits the audience. Sentences flow with a definite purpose and rhythm. Descriptions provide significant details. Sentences are alive. There are no mixed metaphors, misplaced modifiers, redundancies, or words that clutter.	Word choice is accurate but without variety. Word choice doesn't precisely fit the audience. Verbs are static. There are occasional errors in sentence structure.	Word choice doesn't fit the audience. The syntax is choppy, or the sentence structure does not vary. Extensive use of passive voice. Story could be substantially better.
Adequate proofreading.	Only two or three minor errors in spelling or punctuation. Author has proofread drafts and corrected grammatical mistakes.	Story is understandable but has a few too many spelling and punctuation errors.	Sentence structure affects clarity. Numerous mechanical errors.

Take Classes

Be a lifelong learner and take classes regularly to improve your writing skills. Every writing teacher has a different approach; take more than one class to learn different ways to tackle your projects. Ask any friends who have taken classes for recommendations. Make friends with the other students in the class, and if it seems right, consider starting a critique workshop with the other students.

Work with Friends and Colleagues

Ask friends to review and critique your work. Offer to review theirs as well. If others ask you to review their work, ask them if there's anything in particular they want you to look over. Sometimes a friend might ask you to really be tough on the work. Rip it to shreds. But they don't really mean it, and if you do tear apart the work, they will feel bad. Make sure you understand the expectations for any work you review, and set expectations when someone reviews your work.

Your Name Is on the Work

Sometimes a critique can be off or send you in a direction that's not healthy for the story. Make sure you pay attention to your gut instincts and don't just accept any criticism given. Occasionally, an author in a critique group will get stuck on a particular problem and keep reworking a small part of the writing to try to please the critique group. Even when a review comment is from your boss or your teacher, you need to make sure you rewrite the story so that it works best for you and the intended audience.

After you receive a set of comments from your group, don't jump in and start to edit. Take your time. Let the comments rest a day, just as you let the story rest. Read all of the comments again when you've distanced yourself from the critique session. Carefully weigh how you will rewrite your story with regard to the feedback.

Writing takes a thick skin and a sensitive ear. You have to know which comments to listen to and which comments to ignore. You have to know how to listen to your own words.

When Is Your Story Finished?

Most times, you won't feel that you've done all you can for a story, and it won't feel finished. Rarely after a final edit will you sigh with pleasure and delight, feeling completely satisfied with the final product. There's always a sentence that hasn't come to life, a word that doesn't fit, or dialogue that doesn't feel true. Frequently, you'll have more of a feeling that you've run out of time and energy, and abandoned the story so you could move forward to the next one.

Imagination is more important than knowledge.

—Albert Einstein

Challenges

The best way to get better at writing Web content is to write, write some more, and rewrite. The challenges in this chapter focus on gaining a new perspective and rewriting.

Freewriting

The freewriting challenge in this chapter asks you to practice writing using your own writing process with revision in mind.

Freewriting works best when it is timed. If you tend to write quickly, set the timer for ten minutes. If you tend to take a little more time, give yourself 15 minutes. Remember that with freewriting you don't need to worry about accuracy, grammar, spelling, and so forth.

LIKE THE BACK OF MY HAND

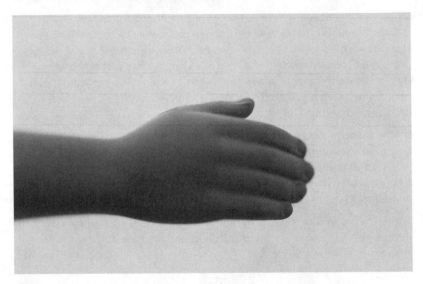

You've surely heard the saying "I know it like the back of my hand." It means you truly know something, just like you know the back of your hand. But do you really know the back of your hand? There are two ways to tackle this writing prompt. You can describe the back of your hand from memory. (Don't cheat and look at it.) Or, if that doesn't appeal to you, write about something that you know so well that you know it like the back of your hand.

Suggested Exercise

Exercises are longer projects that will take more time to complete. You can find more complete instructions, learning outcomes, and criteria for critiquing your work at www.write4web.com.

RE-ENVISION YOUR WORK

Select any exercise from this book that you've already completed but would like to work on again. Take a fresh look at the initial draft, and then rewrite it until you're satisfied that it represents your very best work.

Up Next

With the information in this chapter and the previous chapters, you should now have all the tools, guidelines, and pointers you need to write effective, compelling Web content. The next chapter, "Writing Practice," includes additional free-writing prompts and suggested exercises. Keep writing!

14

Writing Practice

This final chapter includes additional writing challenges that have been tested on hundreds of college students and have produced excellent results.

If a particular challenge doesn't resonate with you, twist it or change it in any way that works best. Stretch beyond your comfort zone. For the freewriting, feel free to use tongue-in-cheek, satire, hyperbole, fiction, or an unreliable narrator. (Unreliable narrators tell the story in ways you can't trust, with lies, biases, and misleading information. They might be inebriated or mentally ill. They are typically unstable and emotional. Part of the fun in reading such a story is piecing together the truth and figuring out why the narrator tells such a confusing story.)

The challenges in this chapter include:

- Freewriting
- Collaborative writing
- Suggested exercises

Freewriting

Freewriting works best when it is timed. If you tend to write quickly, set the timer for ten minutes. If you tend to take a little more time, give yourself 15 minutes. Remember that with freewriting you don't need to worry about accuracy, grammar, spelling, and so forth.

Self-reflection

Write a brief summary that describes where you are in your writing today. What are your main strengths as a writer or artist? Where do you think you need to improve? What is your experience with writing for the Web? If you took a class called "Writing for the Web," what would you hope to take away from it?

Storyboard Your Weekend

Design a storyboard that reflects a story about something you did or something that occurred last weekend. You can find more information about storyboards in Chapter 4, "Adding Motion."

In Case of Fire

A wildfire is raging toward your community, and the police are on your street shouting with bullhorns. You must evacuate! What five personal belongings will you pack in your car before leaving your home? (Assume that your family and pets are safe.)

Zoom In

Write about any situation from a magnified, close-up perspective. You might write about a close call. Use the first person point of view.

Zoom Out

Describe a situation or a place from a distant perspective. For example, you might describe how a city appears while flying over it in an airplane. Use the third person point of view.

My Invention

Have you ever invented anything? Do you have a recipe you invented? Describe your invention and what prompted you to create it.

Danger

Write about any activity that you have taken part in that felt dangerous. Describe why it seemed dangerous. Was it fun? Do you still take part in that activity? Does someone urge you to stop? If you have stopped the activity, explain why.

15 Minutes of Fame

Andy Warhol is famous for saying, "In the future, everyone will be world-famous for 15 minutes."

What will you be famous for? What would you like to be famous for? For this exercise, don't put any limitations on yourself. If you want to be a superhero, a billionaire, or fly to the moon, write about that desire. If you never want to be famous, explain why.

Magic Box

If you had a magic box that refilled itself every time you closed the lid, what would you want to keep in it and why?

At the Airport

Schiphol Airport in Amsterdam is a pleasant place to wait for your next flight because it has plenty of amenities and cozy places to rest. Many airports, however, don't have such comforts. Write about either a pleasant or unpleasant experience you've had in an airport, train station, or bus terminal.

Understand Our Nation

Read the following quote by Robert Thompson, a pop-culture guru and professor at Syracuse University:

"To understand the history of this nation, you have to understand its presidents and its wars. But you also need to understand its lawn ornaments and its cheeseburgers."

Think for a minute about what you might say instead of "lawn ornaments" and "cheeseburgers." For example, you might say, "But you also need to understand its cars and self-help books."

Now it's your turn. Write down what you think needs to be understood to understand our nation. Then continue writing, explaining your answer. Use powerful verbs, and replace any form of "to be" with an active verb.

Family Tradition

Describe a family tradition that you find special. Is it a typical tradition or unusual?

Blackout

Have you ever experienced a blackout in which power went out for an extended period of time? Where were you when the lights went out? Were you driving and perhaps didn't know what happened until you arrived at your destination? What was it like? What did you notice about others around you? Were they polite? Scared? Impatient? What did you do during the long hours of darkness? How did you see? Did you light candles? Use flashlights? Did you feel prepared? Were you worried that the blackout was caused by a terrorist attack?

My Song

Do you have a favorite song? Or, perhaps you know a song that when you listen to it, you say, "That's me!"

Describe your song and why it fits you.

Metaphor

If you were to choose a metaphor that describes you, what would it be? For example, "I am a skateboard," or "I am an electric guitar," or "I am a cheetah." Describe why you chose your metaphor.

Scary, Scary Night

Write about a time you and a friend were really scared. Where were you? What scared you? Did you run away? How did you calm your fear?

Another option is to write a ghost story you told or heard when you were a teenager. Make sure you include the scary sound effects: noises in the basement, heavy footsteps, and creaking doors.

I Have a Dream

Martin Luther King Jr. is remembered for his famous speech in which he repeatedly said, "I have a dream." Repeating a phrase over and over again can give your story strength, cadence, and symmetry. It is a technique that works well for written as well as spoken words.

Listen to Martin Luther King Jr.'s speech on the Web at http://ia600402. us.archive.org/29/items/MLKDream/MLKDream_64kb.mp3.

In addition to "I have a dream," the many phrases he repeats include:

- One hundred years later...
- Now is the time to...
- We can never be satisfied, as long as...

Write several paragraphs, repeating one of Martin Luther King Jr.'s phrases or words of your choice.

Describe a Place

Think of a place that you know well. It might be the kitchen in your childhood home, the branches of a tree you loved to climb, the library, a shop, a beach, or a favorite hangout. Write a few paragraphs describing the place.

Describe a Costume

Think about all the costumes you've ever worn for Halloween, come-as-you-are parties, plays, and so forth. Try to recall your very first Halloween costume or the earliest one that you can remember.

Choose a favorite costume or one that you really hated. How did it feel to wear that costume? Were you transformed into another character? How did you acquire the costume? Did someone make it for you? Did you make it? Did you purchase it? Did someone give it to you?

Write a few paragraphs describing the costume and the event that you wore it to.

Makes Me Mad

Have you ever noticed while driving that you think anyone going faster than you is a maniac but anyone going slower is a putz?

As we navigate through the daily events in our lives, we push our way through crowds, stand in lines, risk life and limb on the freeway, and sit in rooms with odd strangers.

Write about some behavior that makes you mad, contrasting it with the exemplary comportment or demeanor you'd rather experience.

Time Machine

Pretend that you have a time machine that will send you to any place and any time, past, present, or future. Which time period would you choose?

Collaborative Freewriting

The following challenges work best if you write them as a collaborative effort with other authors. They are designed for impromptu writing and will take approximately 25 minutes. Before you begin writing, take the time, as a group, to discuss strategies. Decide on a name for your group to instill teamwork. Choose a team leader, and make sure every member of the group takes part in the collaboration.

Write Instructions

Write instructions for the following topics. Remember that your readers will follow instructions that involve movement more easily if you include images. (Hand-drawn sketches are fine for freewriting.) Also, remember that you'll need to test the instructions. For more information on writing procedures, see Chapter 11, "Writing Instructions."

PAPER AIRPLANE

As a group, decide on a design for a paper airplane. Write the instructions using images and text.

HOW TO JUGGLE THREE BALLS

Find and watch a demo on YouTube on how to juggle three balls. Then write the instructions using images and text.

Game Scenes

Designing a video game takes an intense mastery of several multimedia disciplines. You need a good, interactive story with all the story elements: setting, themes, backstory, characters, plot, dialogue, and interactivity. Games typically have puzzles to solve and missions built into the story as well.

For this exercise, write a brief summary that describes the elements of a game. Choose any of the following suggestions, or make up your own setting, characters, and audience.

HAUNTED HOUSE

Write a game scene with the following elements:

- **Audience.** Tweens
- **Setting.** A haunted Victorian house
- **Characters.** Player, villain, athlete, owner of the house, fitness instructor
- **Goal.** To stay out of harm's way and outsmart the villain by solving puzzles, staving off menaces, and figuring out how the other characters can help

CASTLE MOAT

Write a game scene with the following elements:

- **Audience.** Teenagers
- **Setting.** Medieval castle
- **Characters.** Player, knight, jester, princess, villain, king, queen
- **Goal.** To keep the enemy out of the castle and to find treasures in the moat

HERO'S JOURNEY

Write a game scene with the following elements:

- **Audience.** Young adults
- **Setting.** The Aegean Sea
- **Characters.** Odysseus, Penelope, nymph Calypso, sirens, Cyclops, Charybdis (vortex monster in the sea), Circe (a witch who transforms her enemies into animals). (In *The Odyssey*, all of Odysseus's men become swine.)
- **Goal.** To get Odysseus back home to Penelope.

Student Fool's Day

Write a press release for your school that could be plausible but is actually complete fiction.

The following are examples of scenarios that might work:

- Meet our new mascot—a platypus
- Math student wins an Oscar for Best Actor
- Students pool for tickets and win the lottery

Use the following typical format for your press release.

PRESS RELEASE FORMAT

Contact Information:
  Name
  Address
  Phone
  Email

TITLE OF PRESS RELEASE
City, Month, Day, Year – Lead-in sentence and first paragraph
Second paragraph
Additional paragraphs
Concluding paragraph

Survival Tips for Students

Collaborate on a short blog that offers advice for new college students.

Write a brief introduction that describes your task and any general advice your team agrees upon. Using bullet points for brevity, write down six or seven strategies or tips. Then write a one-sentence conclusion.

Suggested Exercises

Exercises are longer projects that will take more time to complete. You can find more complete instructions, learning outcomes, and criteria for critiquing your work at www.write4web.com.

Artist's Statement

An artist's statement offers a glimpse of your world at the current moment in time. It is not a resume, a bio, or a list of your accomplishments. Rather, it is a summary of your current passions and interests that are relevant for your target audience.

The statement might include descriptions of:

- Your passions
- Your creative process
- Your visions

- Your inspirations
- Your philosophies
- Your likes and dislikes

To write your artist's statement, start by looking over the work you've done recently. Was anything especially easy or hard? What are you most proud of? Least proud of? Are there common themes? Did you find you had a message or important story to tell?

Pretend that you are filming a documentary of yourself. Look into the camera and make a statement about what has influenced you. What are your goals for the future? Did you find a voice that worked well for your writings? A topic you liked best?

Write an Ad

Write an ad for a fictional product, such as:

- A new car that runs on water
- An energy drink made from cactus juice
- A new fragrance designed by your favorite musician

Describe who the target audience is. Keep in mind that most ads have four main goals:

- Get attention
- Arouse interest

- Create desire
- Demand action

Post a Blog

Choose one of the following topics and write a short blog. If none of these topics work for you, make up your own:

- Were you ever seriously addicted to a video game? What was it, and what did you do?

- Is the video game rating system helpful? Many kids are playing games rated M for mature. Do you have any suggestions for changes to make sure children play and enjoy games that are appropriate for their age?

- Mahatma Gandhi practiced *ahimsa*, which means nonviolence. If he were to design a video game, what would it be like?

- Why is football such a different sport in the United States compared to most other countries? If you watch football players in other countries, you can't help but notice how they dance across the field with a soccer ball, whereas in the American sport they rush headlong into the defense and often get trampled.

- Do you like fantasy football? Why?

- Who is your favorite musician and why?

- What activities at your school do you most enjoy?

- Lady Gaga is famous for the fashion statements she makes with her outfits. Do you think this has any effect on her music? How do Lady Gaga's fashion statements compare with those of other female singers, such as Madonna or Cher?

- When guests visit your city and ask for recommendations for things to do and see, what do you tell them? Write a blog that offers suggestions for places to visit for someone who is visiting your city for only one day.

College Reporter

Imagine you work for your college newspaper. Your editor has sent you on assignment to interview students on campus and write a feature story called "Technology and Design." You interview faculty, students, assistants, and administrators. Before sitting down to write the story, you decide to lead by setting the scene. Choose any place on campus and immerse yourself in the details of the location.

Use all five senses to list details about the place, its inhabitants, and any activities that occur. Elements might include answers to the following:

- What does the setting look like? What materials were used in its construction? How traditional or modern does it look? Does it overshadow the occupants?

- How does it sound? Is the space insulated from outside sounds or not?

- Is there any furniture? Are the furnishings purposeful or decorative? Are they aesthetically pleasing or are they utilitarian?

- What activities take place in this space?

Bibliography

For a more detailed list of resources, including book reviews, see www.write4web.com.

Ament, Vanessa Theme. *The Foley Grail: The Art of Performing Sound for Film, Games, and Animation*. Burlington, MA: Focal Press, 2009.

Aristotle. *On Poetry and Style*. Translated by G.M.A. Grube. Indianapolis: Hackett Pub. Co., 1989.

Aronie, Nancy Slonim. *Writing from the Heart: Tapping the Power of Your Inner Voice*. New York: Hyperion, 1998.

Bly, Carol. *Beyond the Writers' Workshop: New Ways to Write Creative Nonfiction*. New York: Anchor, 2001.

Burroway, Janet. *Imaginative Writing: The Elements of Craft*. New York: Longman, 2003.

Butler, Robert Olen, and Janet Burroway. *From Where You Dream: The Process of Writing Fiction*. New York: Grove Press, 2005.

Cameron, Julia, and Michael Toms. *The Well of Creativity*. Carlsbad, CA: Hay House, 2001.

Cameron, Julia. *The Artist's Way: A Spiritual Path to Higher Creativity*. New York: Jeremy P. Tarcher/Putnam, 2002.

Center for Digital Storytelling. www.storycenter.org.

Cooper, Alan. *The Inmates Are Running the Asylum: Why High-Tech Products Drive Us Crazy and How to Restore the Sanity*. Indianapolis: Sams, 1999.

Crews, Frederick. *The Random House Handbook*. New York: McGraw Hill, 1991.

DeSalvo, Louise. *Writing as a Way of Healing: How Telling Our Stories Transforms Our Lives*. New York: Harper Collins, 1999.

Epel, Naomi. *Writers Dreaming*. New York: Carol Southern Books, 1993.

Garrand, Timothy. *Writing for Multimedia and the Web, Third Edition: A Practical Guide to Content Development for Interactive Media*. Burlington: Focal Press, 2006.

Gelb, Michael. *How to Think Like Leonardo da Vinci: Seven Steps to Genius Every Day*. New York: Bantam Dell, 2004.

Glebas, Francis. *Directing the Story: Professional Storytelling and Storyboarding Techniques for Live Action and Animation*. Burlington: Focal Press, 2009.

Goldberg, Natalie. *Wild Mind: Living the Writer's Life*. New York: Bantam Books, 1990.

Goldberg, Natalie. *Writing Down the Bones: Freeing the Writer Within*. New York: Random House, 1986.

Hollander, John. *Committed to Memory: 100 Best Poems to Memorize*. New York: Riverhead Books, 1996.

Holtz, Shel, and Ted Demopoulos. *Blogging for Business: Everything You Need to Know and Why You Should Care*. Chicago: Kaplan Publishing, 2006.

Kelby, Scott. *The Digital Photography Book*. Vol 1. Berkeley: Peachpit Press, 2006.

Keyes, Ralph. *The Courage to Write: How Writers Transcend Fear*. New York: H. Holt, 2003.

King, Stephen. *On Writing: A Memoir of the Craft*. New York: Scribner, 2010.

Krug, Steve. *Don't Make Me Think: A Common Sense Approach to Web Usability*. Berkeley: New Riders, 2000.

Lambert, Joe. *Digital Storytelling: Capturing Lives, Creating Community*. Berkeley: Digital Diner Press, 2002.

LaMott, Anne. *Bird by Bird: Some Instructions on Writing and Life*. New York: Anchor, 1995.

Langan, John. *College Writing Skills with Readings*. New York: McGraw Hill, 2008.

Lederer, Richard. *The Miracle of Language*. New York: Pocketbooks, 1999.

Le Guin, Ursula K. *The Wave in the Mind: Talks and Essays on the Writer, the Reader, and the Imagination*. New York: Random House, 2004.

Le Guin, Ursula K. *Steering the Craft: Exercises and Discussions on Story Writing for the Lone Navigator or the Mutinous Crew*. Portland, OR: Eighth Mountain Press, 1998.

Maisel, Eric. *The Creativity Book: A Year's Worth of Inspiration and Guidance*. New York: J.P. Tarcher/Putnam, 2000.

Maisel, Eric. *Fearless Creating: A Step-by-Step Guide to Starting and Completing Your Work of Art*. New York: Putnam, 1995.

McKee, Robert. *Story: Substance, Structure, Style and The Principles of Screenwriting*. New York: ReganBooks, 1997.

Meadows, Mark Stephen. *Pause and Effect: The Art of Interactive Narrative*. Berkeley: New Riders, 2002.

Miller, Henry, and Thomas Moore. *Henry Miller on Writing*. New York: New Directions, 1964.

Milosz, Czeslaw. *Milosz's ABC's*. Translated by Madeline G. Levine. New York: Farrar, Straus, and Giroux, 2001.

Murray, Janet H. *Hamlet on the Holodeck: The Future of Narrative in Cyberspace*. Cambridge: MIT Press, 1998.

Nielsen, Jakob. Jakob Nielsen's Website. www.useit.com.

O'Shea, Samara. *For the Love of Letters: A 21st-Century Guide to the Art of Letter Writing*. New York: Collins Press, 2007.

Price, Jonathan, and Lisa Price. *Hot Text: Web Writing That Works*. Berkeley: New Riders, 2002.

Progoff, Ira. *At a Journal Workshop: The Basic Text and Guide for Using the Intensive Journal Process*. New York: Dialogue House Library, 1975.

Redish, Janice (Ginny). *Letting Go of the Words: Writing Web Content that Works*. San Francisco: Morgan Kaufmann, 2007.

Rilke, Rainer Maria. *Letters to a Young Poet*. Translation by Reginald Snell. Mineola, NY: Dover Publications, 2002.

Sabin-Wilson, Lisa. *WordPress for Dummies: A Reference for the Rest of Us*. Hoboken, NJ: Wiley Publishing, 2008.

Sellers, Heather. *Page After Page: How to Start Writing and Keep Writing No Matter What!* Cincinnati: F & W Publications, 2009.

Stafford, William. *You Must Revise Your Life*. Ann Arbor: University of Michigan Press, 1986.

StoryCorps. http://storycorps.org.

Strunk, William, Jr., and E.B. White. *The Elements of Style*. New York: Longman, 1999.

Tharp, Twyla. *The Creative Habit: Learn It and Use It for Life*. New York: Simon and Schuster, 2003.

Thomas, Abigail. *A Three Dog Life: A Memoir*. New York: Harcourt Brace, 2006.

Ueland, Brenda. *If You Want to Write*. St. Paul: Graywolf Press, 1987.

Welty, Eudora. *The Eye of the Story: Selected Essays and Reviews*. New York: Random House, 1978.

Index